AF817507

Inland Navigation and Integrated Water Resources Management

About the Authors

Maminul Haque Sarker received his graduation in civil engineering from Bangladesh University of Engineering and Technology (BUET). He did his Masters in Hydraulic Engineering (1996) from IHE, Delft, the Netherlands and PhD (2009) from School of Geography, University of Nottingham, UK. He worked at Bangladesh Inland Water Transport Authority (BIWTA) for 12 years (1981 to 1993); he joined the Center for Environmental and Geographic Services (CEGIS) in 1997. Most of his professional life is spent in working with the river morphology. He has several publications in different journals, books and conference proceedings.

Shampa, the youngest author of this book has grown up seeing the capricious behaviour of Ganges- Brahmputra-Meghna which made her enthusiastic in Water Engineering and consciously she received her graduation from BUET (2011). After successful completion of graduation, she has joined Center for Environmental and Geographic Services (CEGIS). She has some publications in different national and international journals and conferences proceedings.

R.M. Nair was Member (Technical) of the Inland Waterways Authority of India (IWAI) in the Ministry of Shipping from 1995 to 2005. He has been instrumental in formulating major policy initiatives in the Indian Inland Water Transport (IWT) Sector, including the IWT Action Plan (1994), and the IWT Vision 2020 (1998), both of which contributed to the Government of India IWT Policy of 2001. He is a member of the Sub-Group on IWT of the National Transport Development Policy Committee (NTDPC). He is a graduate from the University of Kerala and a specialist in hydrography from the National Institute of Hydrography, Goa.

Jakia Akter a graduate from BUET has been working in CEGIS since 2005. She has more than 10 year experience on hydrology and geo-morphology. She worked for Joint Commission for preparing position papers showing sustainable water sharing options of 26 trans-boundary rivers from 2009 to 2011. She was an active member in preparing Haor Morphology report for Haor Master Plan for Bangladesh Haor and Wetland Development Board in 2011. She is currently working on different geo-morphological study related activities of several projects of CEGIS. She has some publications in journals and conferences.

Syed Monowar Hossain has been working in the Inland Water Transport (IWT) sector since 1984. He served in BIWTA as Director and Secretary, and retired from the service of BIWTA in 2011. As the competent authority on behalf of the Government, he was responsible for the working of Bangladesh-India Protocol on IWT. He has participated in all bilateral meetings since 2000 as nodal point. After retirement, he worked with CEGIS and IUCN.

Inland Navigation and Integrated Water Resources Management

Ecosystems for Life: A Bangladesh and India Initiative

Maminul Haque Sarker
Shampa
R.M. Nair
Jakia Akter
Syed Monowar Hossain

IUCN

ACADEMIC FOUNDATION
NEW DELHI
www.academicfoundation.com

First published in 2014
by

ACADEMIC FOUNDATION
4772-73 / 23 Bharat Ram Road, (23 Ansari Road),
Darya Ganj, New Delhi - 110 002 (India).
Phones : 23245001 / 02 / 03 / 04.
Fax : +91-11-23245005.
E-mail : books@academicfoundation.com
www.academicfoundation.com

in association with
IUCN

Disclaimer:
The findings/views/opinions expressed in this book are solely those of the authors and do not necessarily reflect the views of the publisher or the organisations they represent.

Inland Navigation and Integrated Water Resources Management

by Maminul Haque Sarker, Shampa, R.M. Nair, Jakia Akter
and Syed Monowar Hossain

ISBN 9789332701304

Typeset by Italics India, New Delhi.

Cover Photo: Ms. Sushmita Mandal

Printed and bound by The Book Mint, New Delhi.
www.thebookmint.in

Contents

Preface

Ecosystems for Life: a Bangladesh-India Initiative is a civil society led multi-stakeholder dialogue process to promote better understanding and improved management of natural resources in Bangladesh and India.

Bangladesh and India share some of the world's most intricate and complex river systems. The Ganges, Brahmaputra and Meghna Rivers, along with their tributaries, drain an area of about 1.75 million square kilometres and have direct impact on around 620 million people. These great rivers are inseparable from the history and legends of the region, as well as from the people who depend on them for their well-being. At the same time, the rivers face significant issues related to pollution, biodiversity loss, navigability and flooding-issues exacerbated by the challenges inherent in managing trans-boundary ecosystems.

Ecosystems for Life was designed to help deal with these issues by facilitating multi-stakeholder dialogues among civil society actors. This encourages representatives of civil society, academia, the private sector and other organisations from both countries to engage in extensive dialogue and information sharing and, through research, produce timely and relevant recommendations for both policy and cooperative management.

Guided by a Project Advisory Committee comprising prominent professionals, legislators, diplomats and researchers from both Bangladesh and India, *Ecosystems for Life* has focused on five main themes: the links between food security and water productivity for poverty alleviation; the impacts of climate change, adaptation methods and mitigation strategies; convergence of inland navigation and integrated water resource management (IWRM); the links between economic development and environmental security; and improving understanding of ecosystems and habitats, leading to improved conservation of flagship species.

The first phase of the project concentrated on analysis within each thematic area to identify significant issues, research gaps and priority areas for joint research. This analysis and consultation provided a clear agenda for joint research conducted through the formation of Joint Research Teams (JRTs) consisting of researchers from both Bangladesh and India. Researchers used a common methodology for their analysis and developed a joint report.

This publication is a result of joint research conducted on the convergence of inland navigation and IWRM, and it specifically focuses on the links between economic development and environmental security. The waterways between Bangladesh and north-eastern India provide an important means of cheap transport for bulk agricultural and other goods, but they have been affected by hydro-morphological processes and withdrawal of water which has reduced their navigability in many regions, especially during the dry season. Ensuring sustainable navigability through river improvement and conservation efforts is important in securing not just environmental outcomes but also social and economic benefits.

The JRT for this project included experts in the field from Bangladesh and India who worked with a common methodology, and who met several times during the course of the study. The research focused on the sustainability of the international navigation route between Ashuganj and Karimganj in the north-eastern part of Bangladesh and India to determine what physical and policy impediments exist, and to make recommendations on how to overcome them. Based on the analysis of various data sets collected through field survey and other means, the report makes a number of important recommendations for improving navigability, including:

- The importance of regular maintenance and dredging of some parts of the route within an IWRM framework.
- Improvements to navigation aids and safety.
- Amendments to the current protocol on inland water transit (IWT) and trade.

- Ways to enhance the role of the private sector.

This is a timely report given the growing public and political awareness on the importance of IWT, and the vulnerability of key waterways to environmental degradation and misuse. It has been prepared with a view to its use by academics and civil society organisations, but it also contains specific recommendations for public policy changes and improvements which will be made available to relevant government agencies in both Bangladesh and India.

Ecosystems for Life is implemented in Bangladesh and India by country offices of the IUCN—International Union for Conservation of Nature. It commended in mid-2010 and is supported by the Embassy of the Kingdom of the Netherlands.

Acknowledgements

We, the Joint Research Team, express our gratitude to the International Union for Conservation of Nature (IUCN) for entrusting us with this research on “Inland Navigation and Integrated Water Resources Management”.

The guidance provided by Mr Giasuddin Ahmed Choudhury, former Executive Director and Engr Md Waji Ullah, Executive Director, Center for Environmental and Geographic Information System (CEGIS) and Mrs Bhupinder Prasad, Chairperson, Inland Waterways Authority of India (IWAI), in completing the study is highly appreciated. The support provided by the Bangladesh Inland Water Transport Authority (BIWTA) and the IWAI is also greatly acknowledged.

The support from several professionals in conducting the study and preparing this report is also very much appreciated. Special thanks to Mr Mizanur Rahman and Mr Moshiur Rahman for conducting the social survey and also to Ms Asifa Rahman for linguistic editing support.

Acronyms and Abbreviations

BIWTA	Bangladesh Inland Water Transport Authority
BWDB	Bangladesh Water Development Board
BOT	Build Operate and Transfer
CIDA	Canadian International Development Agency
CIWTC	Central Inland Water Transport Corporation
DHV-IWT	Dwars, Heederik and Verhey Consultants-Inland Water Transport
DEM	Digital Elevation Model
d/s	Downstream of a River
FAP-6	Flood Action Plan 6
FPCO	Flood Plan Coordination Organization
KKMRP	Kalni-Kushiyara River Management Project
POL	Petroleum, Oil, Lubricants
IGNR	India General Navigation and Railway Co.
IWAI	Inland Waterways Authority of India
IWRM	Integrated Water Resources Management
IWT	Inland Water Transport
IUCN	International Union for Conservation of Nature
LAD	Least Available Depth
m	Meter
m^3/s	Cubic Meter per Second
NEDECO	Netherlands Engineering Consultants
NWMP	National Water Management Plan
PWD	Public Works Department
SLW	Standard Low Water
SWMC	Surface Water Modelling Centre
u/s	Upstream of a River

Glossary

Boro Crop	Rice grown during winter season
Rabi	Dry season
Class I channel	Least Available Depth (LAD) 3.60-3.90 m, perennial
Class II channel	Least Available Depth (LAD) 2.10-2.40 m, perennial
Class III channel	Least Available Depth (LAD) 1.5-1.80 m, seasonal
Class IV channel	LAD < 1.50m, seasonal
Dry season	3 months: January-March inclusive (According to NWMP, dry season is defined as October-April.)
Monsoon season	3 months: July-September inclusive (According to NWMP, monsoon season is defined as May-September. The definitions of dry and monsoon season have changed for relating the study with navigation purposes.)

List of Tables and Figures

Summary of the Research

"Ecosystems for Life: A Bangladesh-India Initiative" is a project led by the IUCN to promote insight into transboundary issues across the three major river systems: the Ganges, the Brahmaputra and the Meghna. Convergence of inland navigation and IWRM goals is one of the themes of the project. Inland water transport offers an environment friendly alternative in terms of both energy consumption, noise and gas emission. This research focussed on the sustainability of the international navigation route between Ashuganj and Karimganj in the north-eastern part of Bangladesh and India. Inland navigation in the river Kushiyara, especially in the route between Ashuganj and Karimganj, could be an attractive economic activity which may enhance regional cooperation, if the route is restored and maintained properly.

The main objectives of this research are identifying the causes of deterioration of rivers and water traffic as well as identifying approaches for improving and maintaining navigability in line with the principles of IWRM and sustainable navigation.

The study was carried out using an integrated multi-sectorial approach. A number of literatures were reviewed and historical maps, satellite images were analysed to understand the history of navigation and morphology of the study route. Discharge, water level, hydrographic survey charts, social survey data and traffic data were analysed to understand the prevailing morphological processes and water traffic of the river. The findings of these analyses have helped to identify the causes of deterioration of navigability and traffic as well as to find a way to improve the route. CEGIS (2011) has developed a conceptual model to demonstrate the river evolution processes in the depressed Sylhet Basin. This model was also used here for better understanding of the river's behaviour and to identify the cause of deterioration of river navigability. A review of the "Protocol of Inland Water Transit and Trade, 2009" as well as consultations with stakeholders also helped to assess the current state of the protocol routes as well as the hindrances and constraints.

Status of Navigation in Karimganj-Ashuganj Route

Before the advent of roads and railways, this route was used extensively for transport of goods and passengers especially during the British regime. A brief history of navigation in India during the British regime and the recent decades is presented in Annex 2. This route was used to transport cargo from Assam to Kolkata as was done before the partition between India and Pakistan. The route was suspended for transit cargo since 1965 and was only used for internal passengers and cargo. Data from the early 1960s presented by Flood Action Plan (FAP 6) (SNC *et al.*, 1998a) indicated that Indian in-transit cargo was more than one lakh tonne/y (Figure 4.3).

After the Liberation War of Bangladesh, the route was opened under the Protocol Agreement between Bangladesh and India. However, the traffic never recovered as the growth of railway occurred and later roads and centres of economic activities moved from the waterways. Moreover, the downstream of the route started to deteriorate since 1990. Annual cargo transport reduced significantly over time, and stopped altogether in 2010.

Causes of Deterioration of Navigability and Traffic

The navigability in the Kushiyara River has reduced for large vessels of more than two meter draught, the duration of navigability however, has changed over time. Analysis of water level and satellite images suggested that channel changes at the downstream reaches of Ajmiriganj mainly caused the deterioration of navigability. Several changes occurred in the Kushiyara course during the last three decades, such as development of cut-offs at the downstream of Ajmiriganj and upstream of Katkhal, and avulsion of the Kushiyara to link with the Surma from Katkhal to the Dhaki. These processes have had a huge impact on deterioration of navigability of the river. The Kushiyara River is heavily loaded with sediment. It is likely that the sediment laden flow may cause frequent cut-offs or avulsion of the river courses. The closure of the Mora Surma in the early 1980s increased the pre-monsoon and post-monsoon flow and may have contributed to the deterioration of the navigability of the Kushiyara River.

The partition between India and Pakistan in 1947 also portioned the rivers between these countries. The river service to Assam using this route was stopped in 1965 when the Indian transit traffic was 115,000 tonne. Although it was reopened in 1973, the traffic never recovered as the growth of railway occurred and later roads and centres of economic activities moved from the waterways (SNC *et al.*, 1998a: 3-25).

Future Development of Kushiyara Route

Future development of the navigability and both passenger and cargo traffic have been assessed under different scenarios such as with autonomous development (without any human interventions and climate change), with human interventions such as the Tipaimukh Dam Project in India and the Kalni-Kushiyara River Management Project in Bangladesh, and with climate change.

For assessing the autonomous development of the navigability and navigation traffic of the Kushiyara River, the prevailing physical condition and traffic conditions are projected. The cut-off or avulsion of the river will occur at the same frequency as it was during the last three decades. It may take the Dhaki Nala one to two decades to complete the avulsion process. Transit traffic will be reduced but domestic traffic may increase in the future

The multi-purpose water resources project is at Tipaimukh on the Barak River 200 km upstream from the border between Bangladesh and India. If the dam becomes operational only for power generation without diverting the water for irrigation, dry season flow in the Kushsiyara River will be increased, which will help to improve the navigability of the river.

The Kalni-Kushiyara River Management Project (KKMRP) proposes a number of engineering interventions for integrated water management in the Sylhet Basin. Dredging and other interventions may bring a benefit for the navigation depending on methodology followed during the implementation.

It is assumed that due to climate change, sea level rise would be 100 cm and rainfall will be increased by 20 per cent and cause 20 per cent increase in flood flow and sediment. The water levels of the Kushiyara River both in dry and monsoon seasons are mainly influenced by the water levels at Bhairab Bazaar. The increases in water level at Chandpur or upstream due to sea level rise will not be limited through back water effects; morphological adjustment processes will also contribute to the increases in water level.

Navigation in Kalni-Kushiyara in the Context of IWRM

The Kalni-Kushiyara is an important habitat for a large variety of animals and plants. Natural water flows without any constraint also promote biological purification processes that contribute to cleaner water in support of life. The means of communication of a large number of people living in the Sylhet Basin are fully dependent on navigation during the monsoon. Ensuring navigation in the Kalni Kushiyara all-round the year will improve access to more remote areas during post-monsoon and will inevitably generate additional commercial activity. Production of *Boro*, the main crop of the area, will increase as navigation reduces the risks of pre-monsoon flood damage. Drainage improvements in post-monsoon period will also increase land availability for timely plantation of *Boro* crops. Fish production within the channel will increase, especially during the dry season.

Ways to Sustainable Navigation

Inland water transport (IWT) is a competitive alternative to road and rail transport. An efficiently run IWT system has environmental and social benefits over other modes of freight transport. In addition, inland waterway transport ensures a high degree of safety, in particular when it comes to the transportation of dangerous goods. The IWT will become an 'acceptable mode' when the following conditions are met:

IWT-Cost	- Substantially cheaper than road transport. - Comparable with rail.
IWT – Time of	- More than roadway but comparable with rail transportation.
IWT – Reliability	- Same or better than rail.
IWT – Safety of Cargo	- Same or better than rail.

Based on the analysis presented in the report some recommendations are made on improving navigability, amending the provisions of the protocol, improving navigation aids and safety, and increasing private sector participation. All the recommendations are based on the concepts of sustainability and IWRM. Most of the findings of this research should be considered as indicative. However, the findings also provide an outline based on which future research can be carried out.

The constraints of navigation as identified at the downstream of Ajmiriganj, should be removed mainly through dredging. Recurrent maintenance dredging at a limited scale should be carried out at the upstream of Ajmiriganj to maintain perennial navigation in the river and at the same time a study should be taken up to define the recurrent dredging procedure and for managing dredge spoil. Monitoring of the morphological processes and assessment of the Least Available Depth (LAD) through hydrographic surveys should be carried out regularly. Stabilisation and rectification of the river by appropriate river training works should also be taken up as a parallel action. The protocol routes should be extended from Karimganj to Silchar. A mandatory provision should be made for both the countries to install night navigation facilities along the protocol routes. The private sector may undertake a major role in establishing IWT infrastructure. For this purpose, joint ventures between the government and the private sector should increase. Build Operate and Transfer (BOT) projects should operate with long concession periods. Finally, both the government and the private sector should take necessary steps for addressing the gaps in their efforts to enhance regional cooperation.

1

Introduction

1.1 Background

The Ecosystems for Life: A Bangladesh-India Initiative is a project led by the IUCN to promote insights into transboundary issues across the three major river systems: the Ganges, the Brahmaputra and the Meghna. The Convergence of inland navigation and integrated water resources management goals is one of the five themes of the project.

Inland water transport is a competitive alternative to road and rail transport. In particular, it offers an environment friendly alternative in terms of both energy consumption and noise & gas emission. According to the IUCN (2011), ensuring sustainable navigability in rivers through river improvement and conservancy could help secure water for the various functions of a river system bringing economic as well as social and environmental benefits. The requirements for sustainable inland navigation and the goals of IWRM are thus closely linked and converge. In addition, inland waterway transport ensures a high degree of safety. Finally, it contributes to the decongestion of the overloaded road network in densely populated regions. According to recent studies, the total external cost of inland navigation (in terms of accidents, congestion, noise emissions, air pollution and other environmental impacts) are seven times lower than that of road transport.[1]

This research has focused on the sustainability of the international navigation route between Ashuganj and Karimganj in the north-eastern part of Bangladesh and India. Presently, the Kolkata-Karimganj and Karimganj-Pandu are important navigation routes under the protocol between Bangladesh and India on Inland Water Transit and Trade. This route in Bangladesh is considered primarily for Indian transit traffic and the Government of India pays an agreed amount of money to Bangladesh toward maintenance cost. Therefore, sustainability of this route is an important issue for inland navigation for both the countries.

Inland navigation in the river Kushiyara, especially in the route between Ashuganj and Zakiganj, could be an attractive economic activity if the route is restored and maintained properly. It can serve as an important transport link to reach the remotest part of the north-eastern region of Sylhet division of Bangladesh and at the same time for transporting export-import cargo including Indian transit cargo. Moreover, this route has an important role in communication for a large part of the north-east region of Bangladesh. Nearly half of the route was seasonally navigable only in the monsoon a decade ago, but presently the entire route of a length of 296 km (according to the Inland Navigation Map of Bangladesh Inland Water Transport Authority [BIWTA] 2008) remains non-navigable during the lean period (about 7 months)

1.2 Objectives

The main objectives of this research have been to:

- Undertake initial analysis to understand why inland water transport is growing or declining within the region (and sub-regions).
- Review and assess the extent that sustainable navigation principles have been incorporated into relevant legislation and policies in Bangladesh and India.
- Identify the causes of deteriorating conditions of the rivers affecting navigation.
- Identify approaches for improving and maintaining navigability in line with integrated resource management principles.
- Identify the rate of decline/growth of inland water traffic in the study region.
- Identify ways to better incorporate sustainable navigation principles into these regulations.

1.3 Study Area

The research has focussed on the sustainability of the international navigation route between Ashuganj and Karimganj in the north-eastern part of Bangladesh and India (Figure 1.1). Presently, the Kolakta-Karimganj and Karimganj-

1. *http://ec.europa.eu/transport/inland/index_en.htm,* 27th April, 2012.

Figure 1.1

Map Showing the Protocol Navigation Route and Study Area in Bangladesh-India

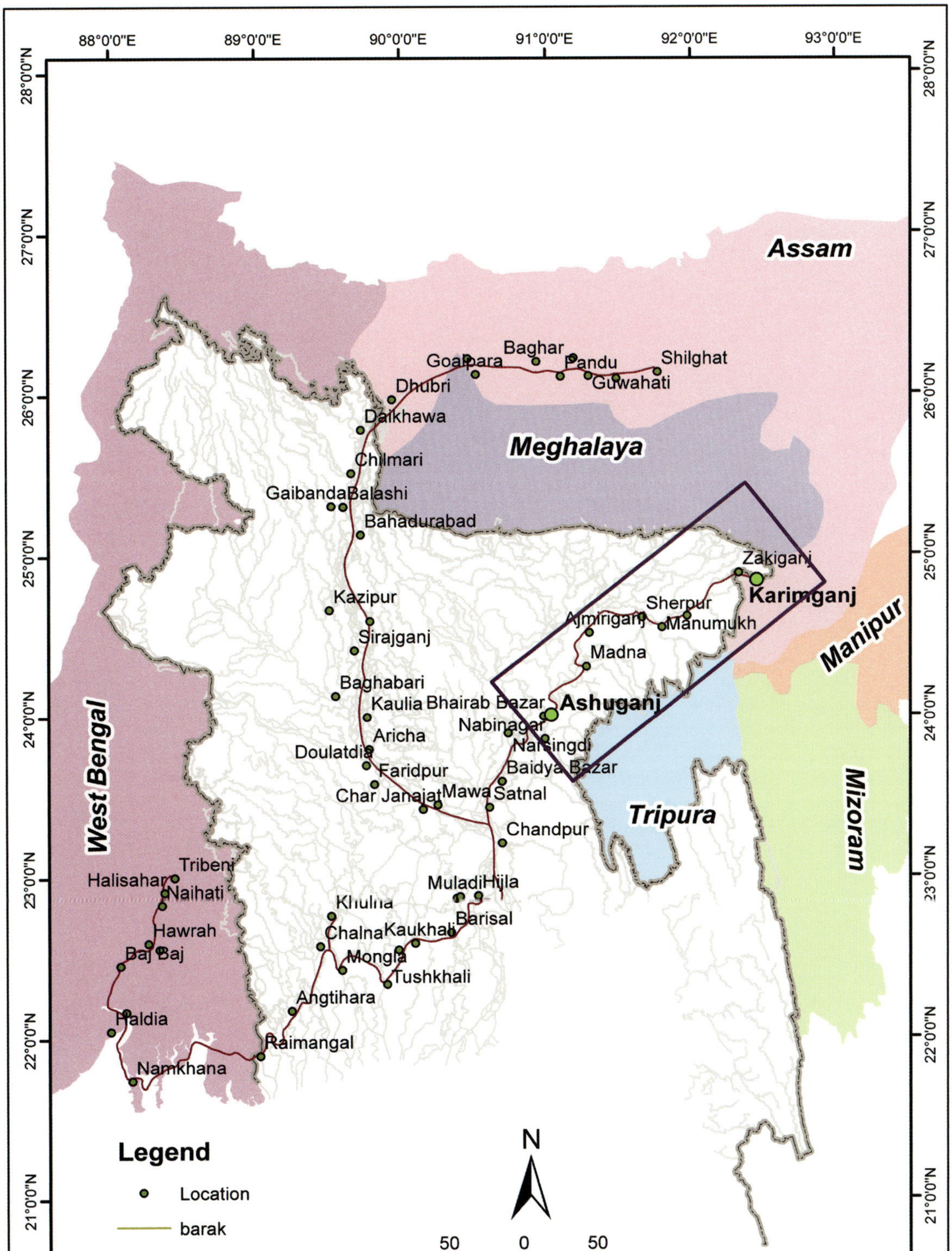

Source: CEGIS, 2011a.

Pandu routes are important navigation routes under the protocol between Bangladesh and India on Inland Water Transit and Trade. Under the protocol agreement between Bangladesh and India, India has annually contributed a fixed amount of money to maintain certain reaches of these routes. The Surma and Kushira rivers also provide connectivity with the hinterland for the intra Bangladesh traffic and this route is the main means of communications for a part of the deeply inundated Sylhet Basin. Therefore, sustainability of this route is an important issue for inland navigation for both the countries.

About a 300 km long reach of this route is in the Kushiyara River with the 20 km downstream reach situated in the Meghna River. The Kalni-Kushiyara River System of the then British Period acts as the inter-regional link for transportation and communication. The downstream reach of the route was fairly navigable throughout the year, but the upstream reach i.e., the Kushiyara River was not perennially navigable for large vessels. Large-capacity vessels used this route from the north-eastern Indian province to Kolkata and Patna during the high stage of the river (stakeholder consultation with Mr Syed Monwar Hossain, former secretary of BIWTA, 2011). Domestic traffic within Bangladesh was also significant. Many mechanised and non-mechanised boats with bulk cargoes of paddy, fertiliser and fish used this route.

This international route was suspended from 1965 to 1972 but has been reopened under the India-Bangladesh Protocol agreement. The navigability of the route started to deteriorate since the end of the 1980s (SNC *et al.*, 1998a: 3-25). Both man-made interventions and natural processes together are probably responsible for the observed deterioration.

1.4 Content of the Book

This report is organised as follows:

- *Chapter-1, Introduction*, presents a background of the study, the objectives and a brief description of the study area.
- *Chapter-2, Data Used*, provides information about the data used in this study and their sources.
- *Chapter-3, Methodology*, gives a brief description of the methodology.
- *Chapter-4, Status of Navigation in the Ashuganj-Karimganj Route*, characterises past and present navigation conditions of the study route.
- *Chapter-5, Geo-morphological Setting and Historical Changes*, describes the salient features of the morphological setting along with the historical shifting processes of the Kushiyara River.
- *Chapter-6, Hydro-morphological Characteristics of the Kushiyara River*, describes the hydro-morphological processes related to the navigability of the Kushiyara River.
- *Chapter-7, Development of Model of Rivers in Sylhet Basin*, presents a model to elucidate the evolution processes of the rivers in the Sylhet Basin so that it can be linked to improve the navigability of the rivers.
- *Chapter-8, Causes of Deterioration*, identifies the causes of deterioration of navigation and traffic.
- *Chapter-9, Future Development*, describes the autonomous development of the route along with human interventions and climate change.
- *Chapter-10, Review of Protocol*, gives an overview of the "Protocol of Inland Water Transit and Trade" between Bangladesh and India. It also defines sustainable navigation and suggests measures to improve the study route as a sustainable one.

2

Data Used

1.1 Data Used

A wide category of data was collected for the study from secondary and primary sources (Table 2.1). The data included spatial data such as historical maps, satellite images and hydrographic charts as well as hydro-morphological data such as water level, discharge, sediment concentration, bed material sizes and socioeconomic data collected through Key Informants Interview (KII) and general consultations. The locations of the hydrological gauging stations of the Bangladesh Water Development Board (BWDB) in the Kalni Kushsiara River are presented in Figure 2.1.

2.2 Key Informants Interview (KII) and General Consultations

KII and general consultations were held in different locations of Bhairab to Zakiganj (Figure 2.2) to gather people's perception about the past and present status of navigability in the Kusiyara River. The consultations were made with local people, BIWTA pilots stationed at Bahirab Bazaar, and BIWTA officials responsible for maintaining the navigation routes. At every location four to seven people were interviewed. The detailed information about this Key Informants Interview is given in Table 2.1. The interviewed people were asked a set of questions (Annex 1) about the available depth for navigation during monsoon and dry season as well as passenger and cargo traffic in the past three decades. They were also asked about the cause of deterioration of the river's navigability and reduction of the number of passengers and cargos, the means of improving the situation and if improved, whether the number of passengers or cargos will increase.

Figure 2.1

Locations of Water Level and Discharge Stations

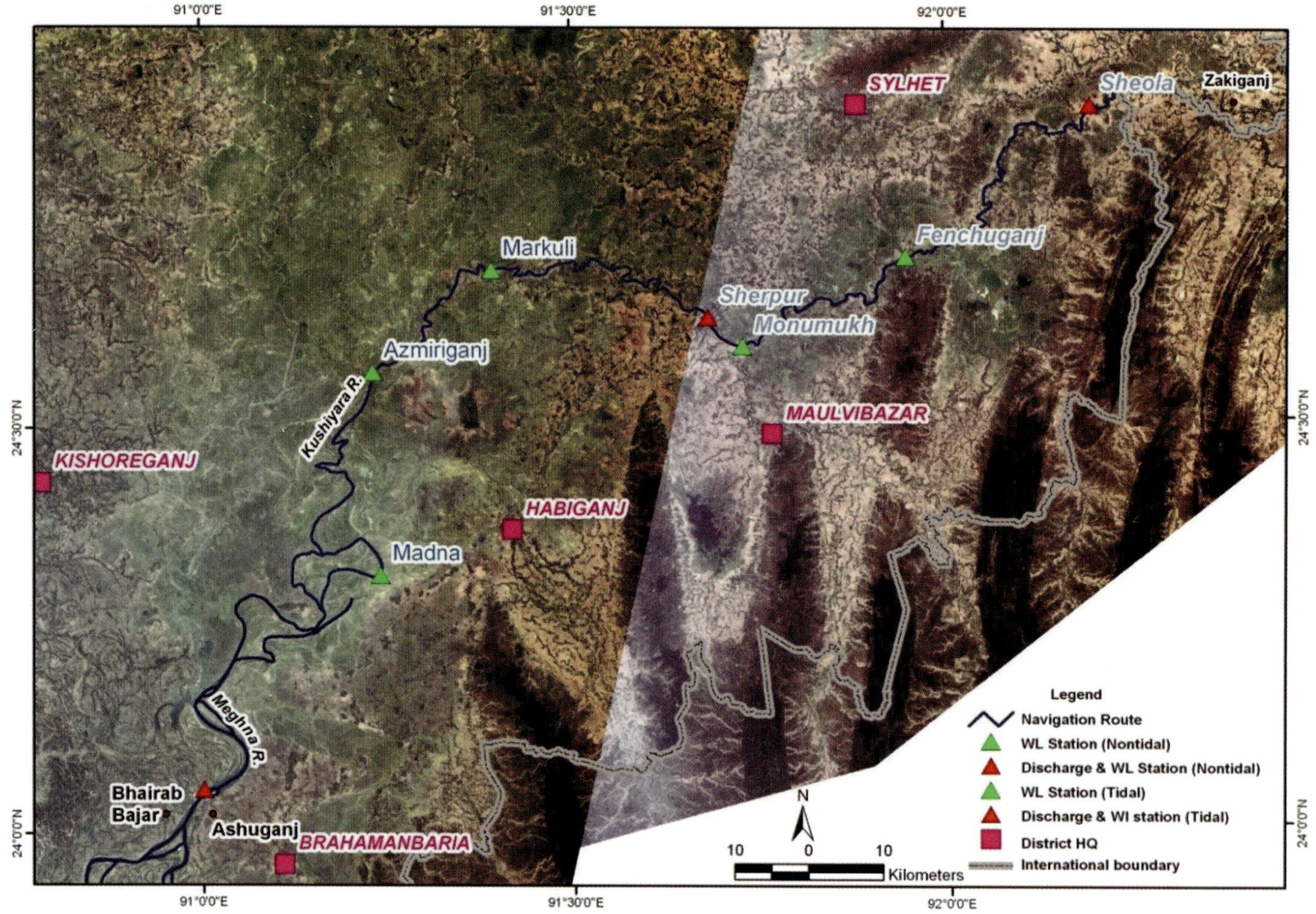

Source: CEGIS, 2011a.

Table 2.1

List of Data

Data	*Source*	*Location/Station*	*Period*
Discharge	BWDB	Sheola Sherpur Bhairab Bajar	1964-2006 1982-2006 1964-2006
Sediment Concentration and Bed materials	FAP 6 CEGIS		1996 2011
Water Level	BWDB	Sheola Fenchuganj Manumukh Sherpur Markuli Ajmiriganj Madna Bhairab Bajar	1950-2009 1949-2009 1959-1983 1982-2009 1956-2009 1956-2009 1949-2009 1949-2009
Hydrographic Charts	BIWTA	Kushiyara river	2005 2006 2010
Satellite Images	CEGIS archive	Kushiyara river	1984 1997 2010
Historical Maps	CEGIS archive	Bangladesh Bangladesh Bangladesh	Rennels Tassins 1943
Socioeconomic Data	Primary	Bhairab Ajmiriganj Markuli Sherpur	2011 2011 2011 2011

Table 2.1

Details of Key Informants Interview

Location	*Type of Waterway User*	*Number of Participants*
Bhairab Bazar	Pilot Co-pilot Master Passager	6 1 1 3
Ajmiriganj	Pilot Business Farmer Gaze rider	1 3 2 1
Markuli	Business Gaze Reader	1 1
Sherpur	Pilot Master	6 2
Fenchuganj	Pilot Master	4 3
Zakiganj	Business Passenger	2 1
BIWTA Officials	BIWTA Director Senior Deputy Director	5 1

Field data, thus collected and analysed, were used to provide information on the relevant aspects.

2.3 Limitations of the Study

The Discharge and Water Level data used in this study were collected from BWDB ranges from 1950 to 2009. There were gaps in the data series. If such gaps are more than 3 days for monsoon (June to September) and 5 days for dry season (January to March) the annual maximum and minimum water level and discharge were not considered for that particular year. Analysis of water level data also showed inconsistency in data series to the magnitude of several tens of centimeters.

A very few sediment samples were collected for this study. The findings of FAP-6 (SNC *et al.*, 1997) study were reviewed for better understanding of the sedimentological processes in the north-east region of Bangladesh. But for proper realisation of the sedimentation processes more data both in dry and monsoon season would need to be collected which was not done for the time constraint of the project.

The cross-section data were taken from BWDB standard cross-section survey. But no recent data was available for Kushiyara River hence cross-section data of 1997-98 was used to assess the bank level profile.

Several satellite images of 30m x 30m resolution were used in this study. These images were geo-referenced using the CEGIS 1997 Landsat Image mosaic. There were some errors that were mainly due to the spatial resolution of the images and maximum value of which would be 1.5 time of the spatial resolution.

The geo-referenced images were used to delineate the banklines of the river. The

Figure 2.2

Locations of Public Consultations held in October 2011

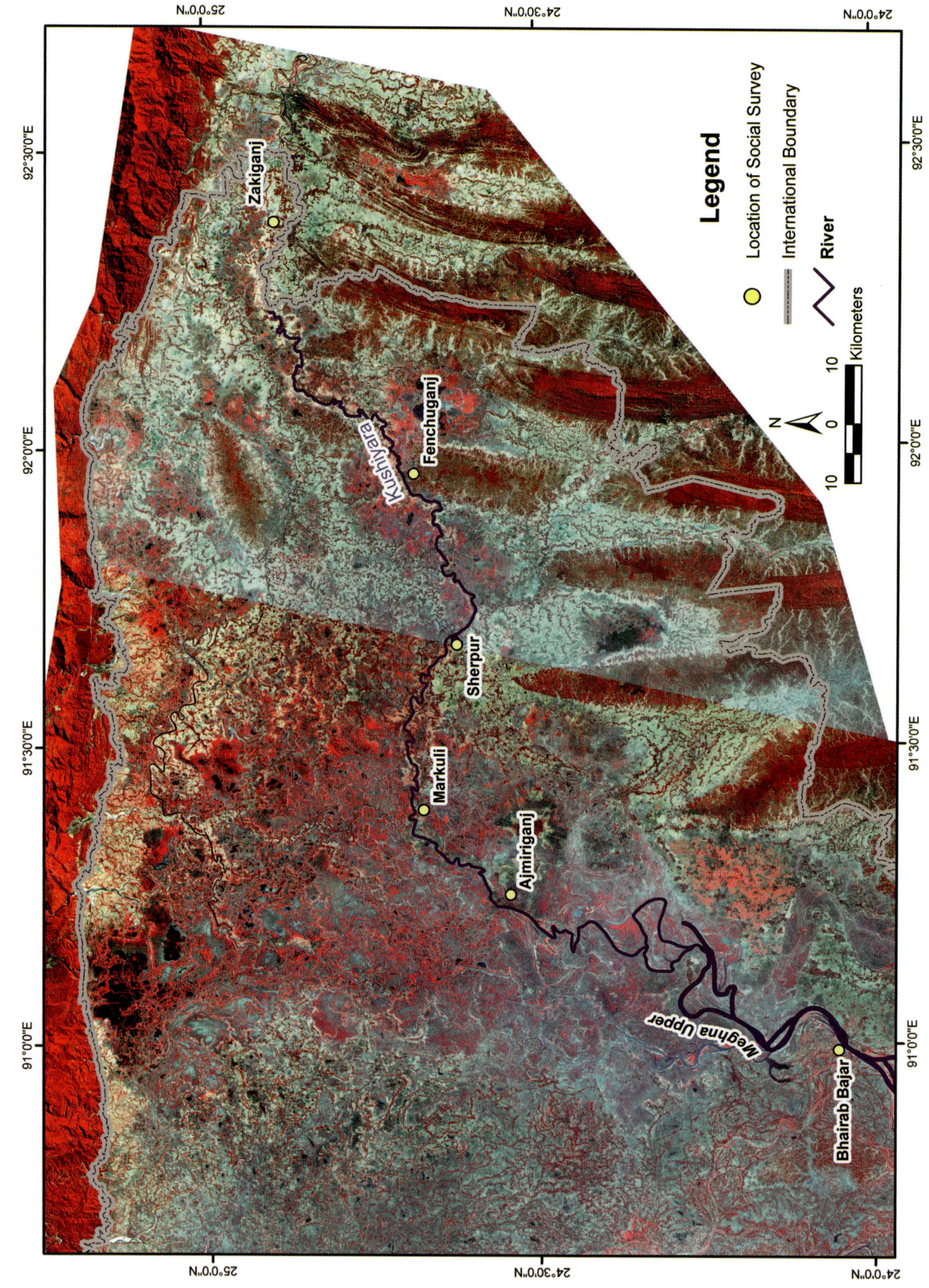

Source: CEGIS, 2011a.

bankline separates the floodplains from the riverbed. All the sand bodies except the crevasse splays (the coarse sediments that are spread over the floodplains during floods by overtopping the banks), are considered to be part of the riverbed. Errors are generated due to the spatial resolution of the images. Bank lines of the Kuhsiyara Rivers are delineated from the satellite images of 1990 and 2010.

Historical maps such as Rennel's (1776), Tassin's (1840) and other maps based on survey of 1909-1930 were used in this study to assess the course changes in Kalni-Kushiyara river system. Attempts were made to geo-reference these maps in a common projection system. There were errors in geo-referencing the old maps, which would be several hundred meters.

3

Methodology

3.1 General Approach

The study was carried out using an integrated multi-sectorial approach. The multi-disciplinary team included: morphologists, water resource engineers, navigation specialists and sociologists. The investigation also included a set of new data.

Most part of the study route falls in the Kushiyara and Upper Meghna rivers. Recent experience of CEGIS, 2011 suggested that the critical reaches for navigation between Ashuganj and Karimganj were mainly in the Kushiyara River. Therefore, analyses of the river data were concentrated on this particular river. A flow diagram of the work is presented in Figure 3.1. The items of work required to achieve the goal are divided into three categories: inputs, analysis and outcomes.

3.2 Input

The Master Plan of the Bangladesh Inland Water Transport Authority (BIWTA) 1989, studies carried out under the framework of the Flood Action Plan for the Northeastern Zone of Bangladesh (FAP-6) 1993-1998, reports of the Center for Environmental and Geographic Information Services (CEGIS) on the Haor Master Plan, 2011, and the report on morphological studies of nine navigation routes, 2011 carried out by CEGIS for the BIWTA were reviewed to understand the morphological behaviour of the Kushiyara River and to identify the causes of the deterioration of navigability in the study route.

Existing navigation arrangements in the protocol routes were studied to identify the areas where improvements were needed. Interactions with trade, shippers and carriers helped to assess their expectations for improved performance and productivity.

The Sustainable Development of Inland Waterway Transport in China, World Bank Report (Paualamos *et al.*, 2009) and the IWT Action Plan (India) 1994 was studied for input on cargo trend and potential, sustainability and international trends in the IWT sector as well as IWT development strategy.

Time-series hydro-morphological data such as on discharge, water level, sediment transport, hydrographic survey charts, satellite images, and secondary traffic data were analysed for this research to assess the causes of the deterioration of navigability in the Kushiyara River.

3.3 Analysis

The most critical reach of the Kushiyara River lies in the subsiding Basin of Sylhet. CEGIS (2011) has indicated that the evolution process of the rivers in such depressed Basin differs in many respects from other parts of the country. Historical maps, time-series satellite images and available Digital Elevation Model (DEM) were analysed to understand the geological and historical nature of the river system. This was helpful in assessing the causes of deterioration in navigability and also for suggesting measures for improving navigability.

Discharge, water level, hydrographic survey charts, satellite images and historical maps were analysed to understand the prevailing morphological processes of the Kushiyara River. Analysis of time-series data revealed the trends in water level, discharge, sediment transport, long-profiles of the river, and least available depth (if it exists). The analysis was also helpful in assessing the causes of deterioration of navigability in the Kushiyara River.

CEGIS (2011) has developed a conceptual model to demonstrate the river evolution processes in the depressed Sylhet Basin after it shifted to its new course. This model has not been calibrated due to a lack of relevant data but has been used in the morphological study for the Haor Master Plan. CEGIS collected data on flow velocity, sediment concentration and bed material samples in the downstream reaches of the Kushiyara River under the framework of this study and used them to support the model. The model was useful in identifying the causes of deterioration of navigability in the Kushiyara River. It also helped in assessing future developments and in planning interventions to improve navigability.

The future development of the study route was assessed by considering autonomous development, the impacts of climate change, and the impacts of human intervention.

A review of the "Protocol of Inland Water Transit and Trade" and relevant documents as well as consultations with stakeholders helped to assess the current state of the protocol routes and the hindrances and constraints.

3.4 Outcomes

The outcomes of the study are: (1) the causes of deterioration of navigability and changes in navigation traffic; (2) recommendations on measures for improving navigability and traffic in line with IWRM principles; and (3) identification of ways to incorporate better sustainable navigation principles.

Figure 3.1

Flow Diagram Showing the Methodology of the Study

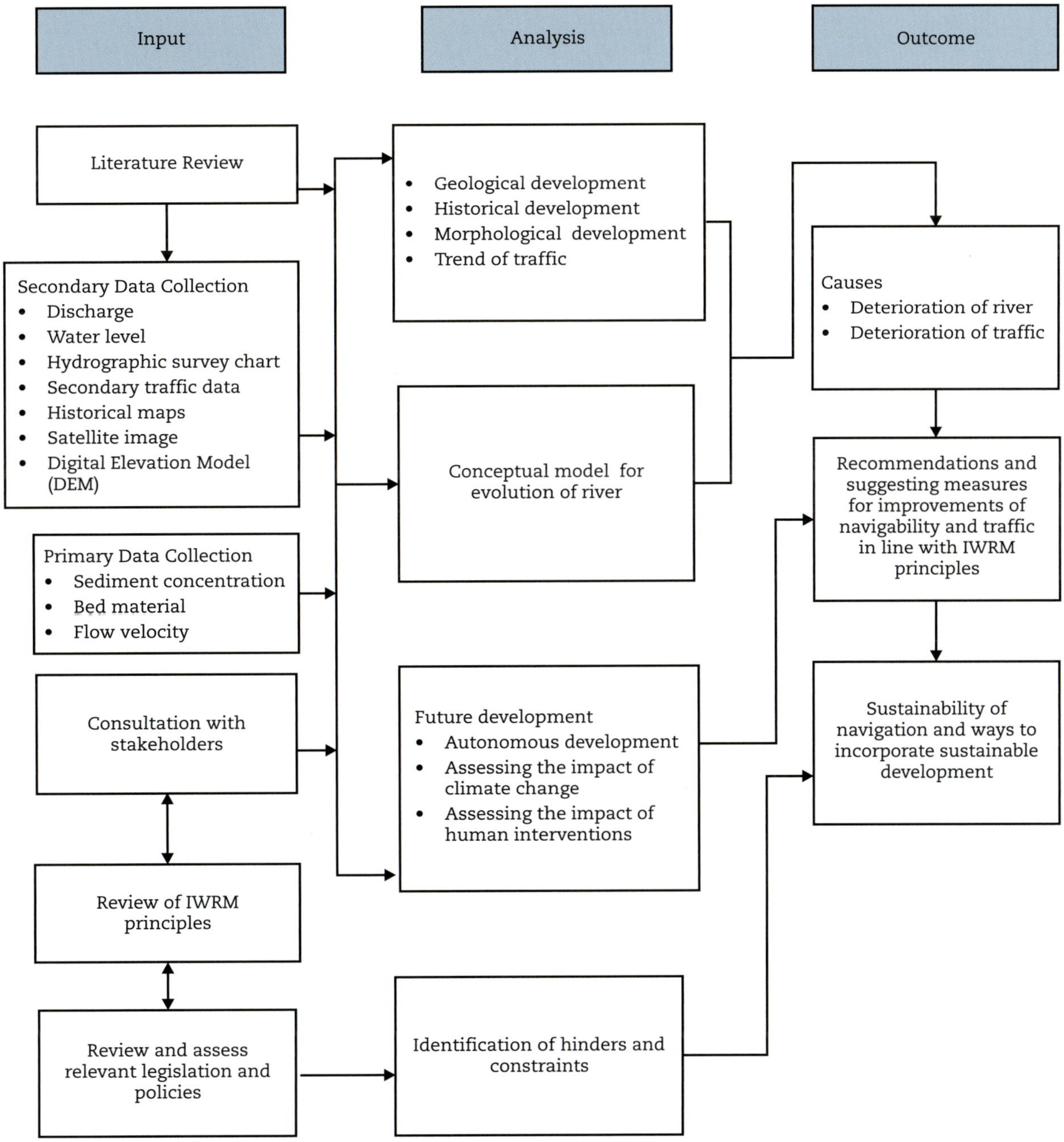

4

Status of Navigation in the Ashuganj-Karimganj Route and Protocol on Inland Water Transit and Trade between Bangladesh-India

4.1 Physical Setting of the Route

Rainfall in the northeastern region of India and Bangladesh is very high. In fact, the world's highest annual rainfall occurs in this region of India at Cherrapunji, Meghalya, very close to the international border between the two countries. There used to be several streams for draining this precipitation to the sea. The Barak is one of the rivers that collect surface run-off from Manipur, Nagaland and Assam. The Barak flow divides into two courses, the Surma and the Kushisyara at Amalshid at the international border. After the division, the Kushiyara flows about 37 km along the international border. Karimganj, an important town in India is situated 12 km downstream of Amalshid on the left bank of Kushiyara River. Zakiganj is situated on the opposite side of Karimganj in Bangladesh which is also an important town (Figure 4.1). The length of the Kushiyara River from Karimganj is 142 km. After meeting with the Mora Surma River at Markuli, the river flows as the Kalni-Kushiyara River. The length of this river is 90 km before it meets with the Surma-Baulai and the combined flow is named as the Meghna (CEGIS, 2011a). A major part of the Kushiyara River lies within the deeply flooded Sylhet Basin (Figure 4.2) where waterways are the main means of communication throughout the year. Therefore, this route is very important to the people living in the Basin area and to Indian in-transit cargo traffic.

Navigability in the Meghna River was perennial and fair all the time. However, navigability of the Kushiyara River was seasonal and the status has been changing over time. The course of the Kushiyara River has been avulsing from the Khatkhal through the Dhaki Nala since the mid 1990s (Figure 4.1). Presently navigability in the old course through the Madna has been reduced. The total length of the route has now become 293 km (CEGIS, 2011a).

4.2 History of Navigation along the Ashuganj-Karimganj Route

Before the advent of roads and railways, rivers were used extensively for transport of goods and passengers. A brief history of navigation in India during the British regime and the recent decades is presented in Annex 2. India's northeastern region consists of 8 states namely the Arunachal Pradesh, Assam, Manipur, Meghalaya, Mizoram, Nagaland, Sikkim and Tripura, occupying 2,62,179 sq. km (North Eastern Region Vision 2020, 2008). One of the key development constraints in the northeast has been its geographical isolation and inadequate connectivity with the rest of India. However, the northeastern region has abundant water resources and several important rivers flow through this region—many of which drain into the Brahmaputra or the Barak which further drain themselves into the Bay of Bengal through Bangladesh. From the colonial period to the present day, several attempts have been made to make this waterway an important route for linkage of the northeast region with the rest of India as well as Bangladesh. For describing the history of navigation of this route, the time is divided into three periods such as British, Pakistan and Bangladesh regimes.

British Regime

Towards the middle of 1800's (Griffiths, 1979) the steamer companies turned their attention to Cachar, where the possibility of tea cultivation had been realised at that time. Cachar was a business hub on the banks of the Barak in Assam. Therefore in 1863, the India General Navigation and Railway Co. (IGNR) despatched the Agra on a voyage to Cachar. The establishment of a monthly service had been contemplated, but the experience of the first voyage showed that the shallowness of the rivers of Cachar in the dry season created considerable difficulties and for some years the IGNR steamers only plied to Cachar during the rainy season.

In 1885 the IGNR, again acting on its own, secured a contract for a despatch service to Cachar. In view of the difficulty of navigating the rivers of Cachar in the dry season, special vessels of shallow draft were required. They could only start from Narayanganj since the coaching traffic between Goalundo and Narayanganj was still under the railway. The terminus of the service was Fenchuganj, but the IGNR also introduced a vessel to link Fenchuganj with the important business centre, Karimganj.

In the year 1900 (Griffiths, 1979) three services operated in Cachar: the Cachar Main Line, the Cachar Despatch and the Cachar Mail (Weekly). They operated from Calcutta to Fenjuganj during low

Figure 4.1

Navigation Route from Ashuganj, Bangladesh to Karimganj, India

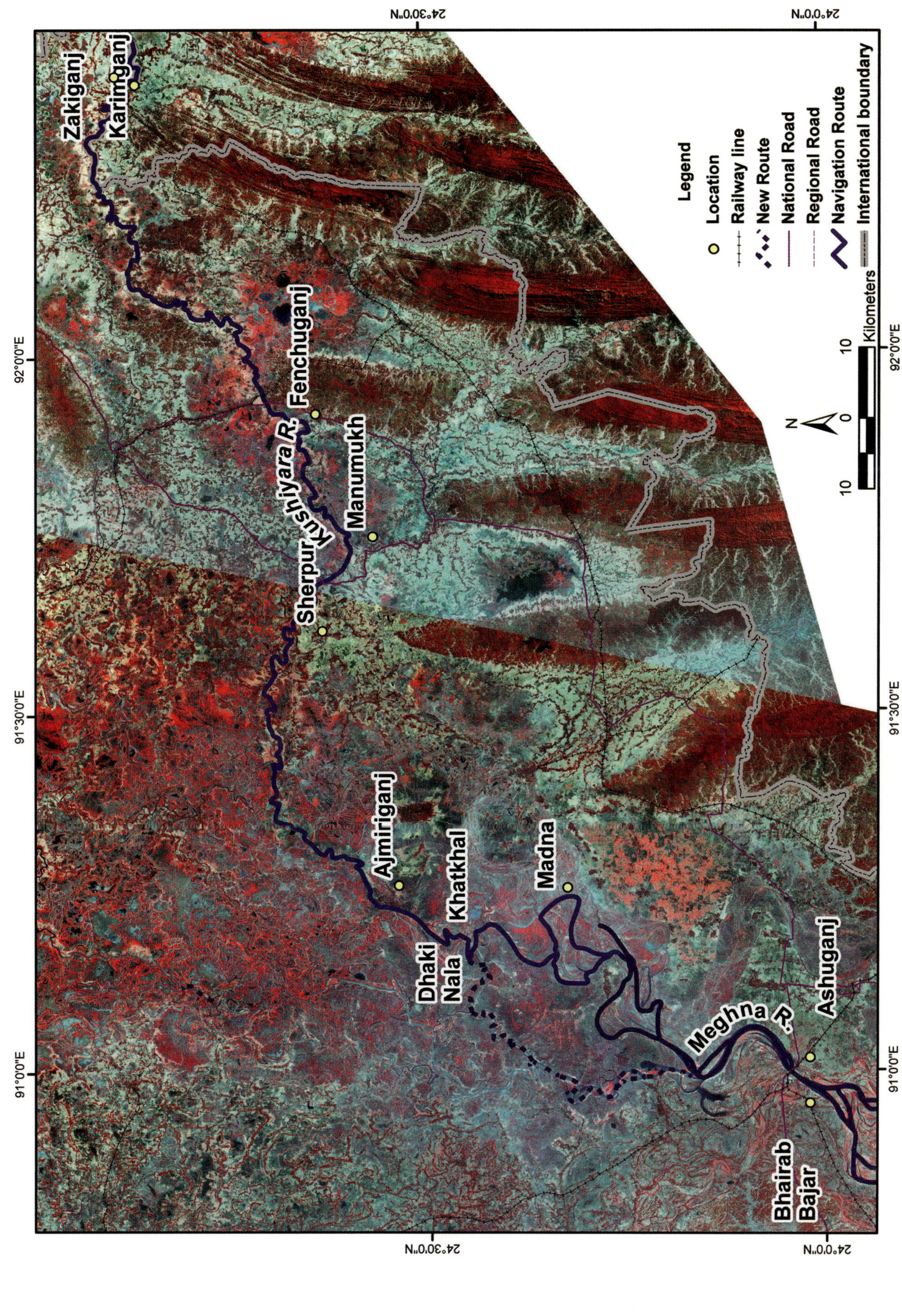

Landsat TM, 30 January, 2010.

Figure 4.2

Incidence of Flood in the Northeast Region of Bangladesh

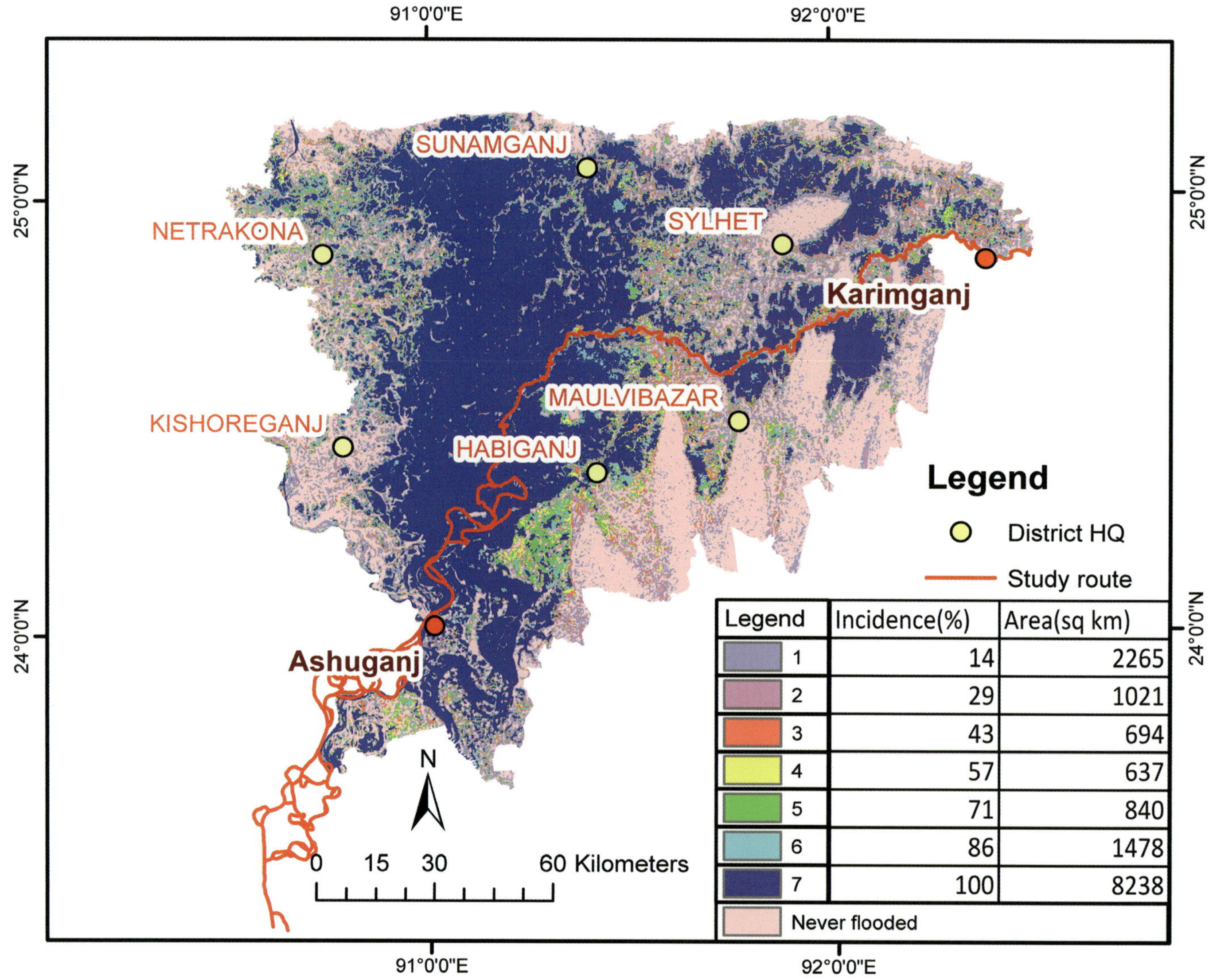

Source: CEGIS, 2011a.

water season and up to Karimganj during rainy season. The feeder routes included Fenjuganj-Karimganj and Fenjuganj–Chatak.

Pakistan Regime

This route was used to transport cargo from Assam to Kolkata as was done before the partition between India and Pakistan. The route was suspended for transit cargo since 1965 and was only used for internal passengers and cargo. NEDECO, an international engineering consulting company classified the Inland Navigation Routes in 1967 based on their importance. The route in the Meghna was classified as Class II, and the route in the Kushiyara up to the confluence of the Monu River was classified as a Class III route. The depth available below Standard Low Water (SLW) was 1.4 m (NEDECO, 1967). NEDECO (1967) also presented their measurement that was done in 1966, which showed that the available depth below SLW varied from 1 to 2 m at different reaches of the Kushiyara River.

Data from the early 1960s presented by FAP 6 (SNC *et al.*, 1998a) indicated that Indian in-transit cargo was more than one lakh tonne/y (Figure 4.3).

Bangladesh Regime

After the Liberation War of Bangladesh the route was opened under the Protocol Agreement between Bangladesh and India. The provisions under the Protocol Agreement, which is a continuation of a signed agreement of 1972, are presented in Annex 3.

The Ashuganj-Karimganj protocol route was never a perennial route. In the 1970s and 1980s, the available depth at the downstream reach of the Kushiyara River up to Sherpur was better than at the upstream. In the IWT Master Plan prepared in 1989 the route was classified as Class III type based on the Least Available Depth (LAD) (DHV *et al.*, 1989). At that time, the LAD from Ashuganj to Zakiganj was 1.5-1.8 m (DHV *et al.*, 1989).

According to BIWTA officials the route was opened for about six months a year, but it started to deteriorate from the 1990s (Stakeholder consultation, Mr Syed Monwar Hossain, 2011). Although the upstream reach of the river improved, the downstream reach deteriorated. The protocol route is now opened only for three months a year. Annual cargo transport also reduced significantly over time. In the 1980s, annual inter-transit cargo was 18 to 38 thousand tonnes (SNC *et al.*, 1998a). After gradual decrease, this amount became nil in 2010 (Stakeholder consultation, Mr Syed Monwar Hossain, 2011).

Although the protocol route is operational only for three months, local cargo and passenger transport continue, as they do not have any other alternative in the Sylhet Basin. A total of 450,000 tonnes of cargo was handled through the Kalni-Kushiyara in 1995 (SNC *et al.*, 1998b). There were significant variations between wet and dry season trade. In 1995, the total number of incoming and outgoing cargo in different reaches in the Kalni-Kushiyara during dry season was 149,330 tonnes and 292,000 tonnes during monsoon. It is to be noted that after the 1990s, the lower reach of the Kalni-Kushiyara has become totally inaccessible to passengers and cargo by formal vessels during dry period, except by mechanised country boats (SNC *et al.*, 1998a). These boats contribute largely in carrying both passenger and cargo. Table 4.1 shows freight traffic of 1995 in the dry season. Rice, fertiliser, and building materials are the main internal cargos in this route. The cargos are mainly transported from Ashuganj to Fenchuganj. In 1995, the total number of annual passengers was 9.70 million of whom 3.30 million passengers made their trips in the dry season and 6.40 million in the wet season (SNC *et al.*, 1998a).

Transit traffic through the Kalni-Kushiyara was up to 113,000 tonne/year in the early 1960s. It remained suspended during the period 1965 to 1973, but after it was reopened under the protocol agreement between Bangladesh and India in 1972 the cargo volume reached only 25 per cent of the previous transit in the 1980s (Figure 4.3) (SNC *et al.*, 1998a). The volume of traffic continued to decrease gradually over time and eventually became very low. The route deteriorated to such an extent by 2011 that the BIWTA did not include it as one of the classified navigation routes (Figure 4.3).

Figure 4.3

Changes in Indian In-transit Traffic through Ashuganj-Karimganj Route Over Time

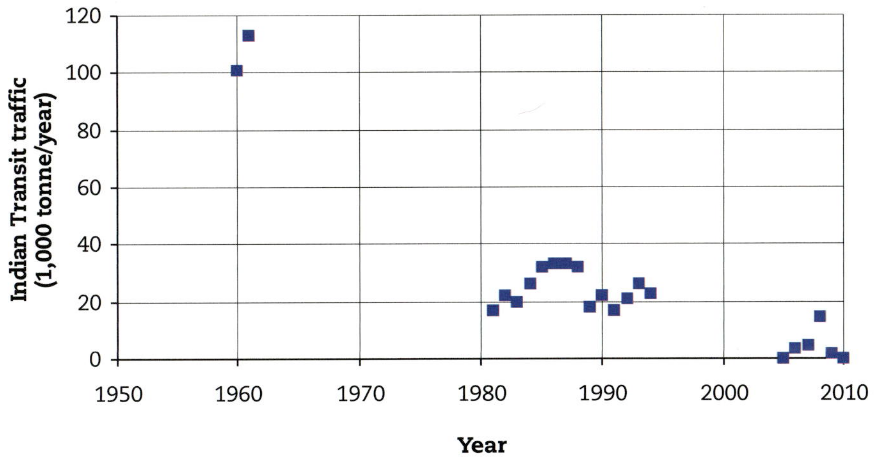

Source: SNC *et al.*, 1998b and BIWTA.

Table 4.1

Freight Traffic in Kalni-Kushiyara

Item	*1995 Traffic ('000 tonnes)*
Fertilizer demand	22
Fertilizer rehandling	2
Fertilizer trans-shipment	28
Rice	30
Building materials	73
POL Urban	3
POL Rural	7
Other food items	20
Consumer goods	31
Internal rehandle	13
Total	229

Source: SNC *et al.*, 1998a.

Figure 4.4

Status of the Study Route in Different Periods

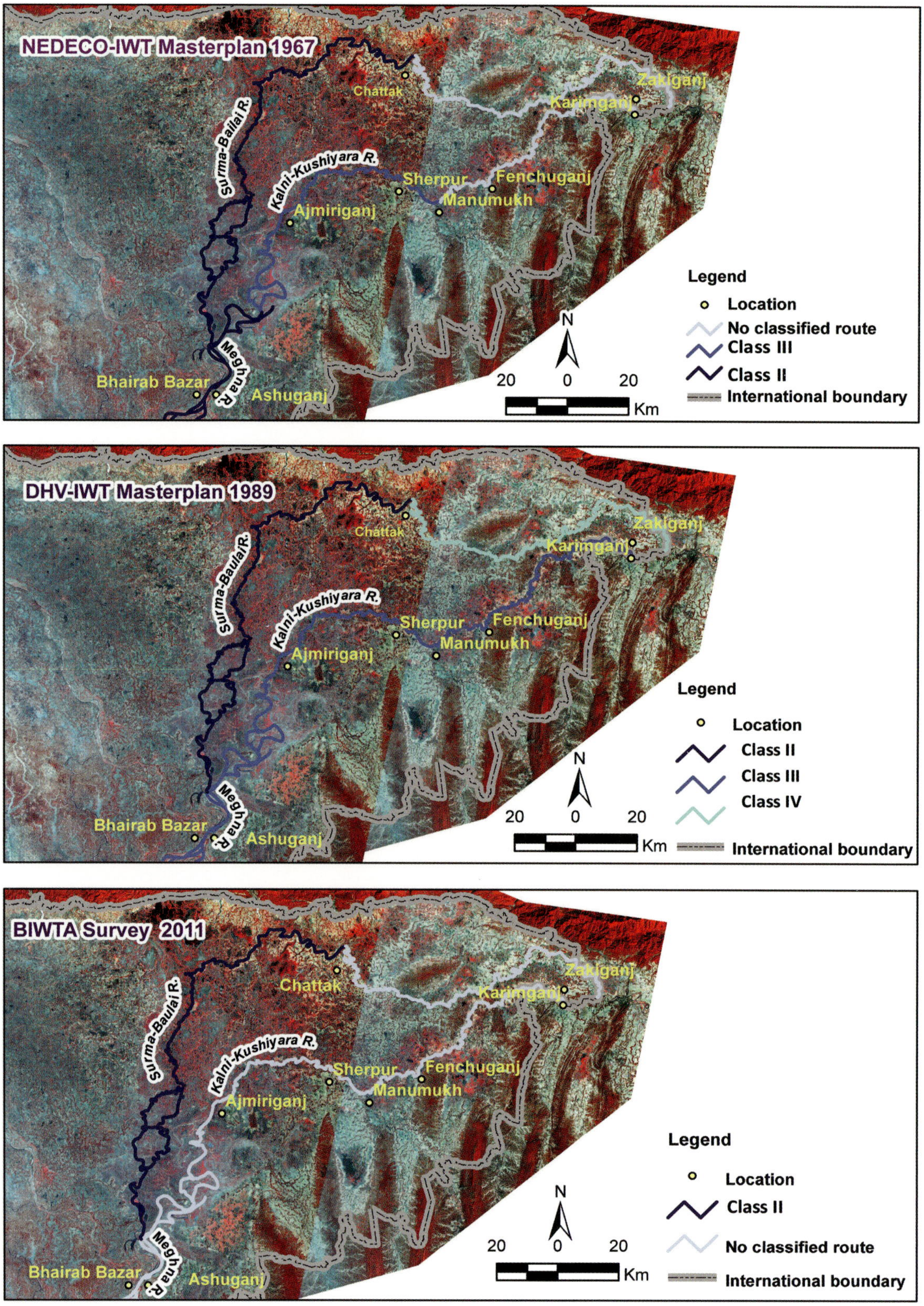

Source: CEGIS, 2011a.

4.3 Salient Features of Bangladesh-India Protocol on IWTT

For better utilisation of transboundary rivers, there exists protocol on inland water transit and trade so that inland vessels of one country can transit through the specified routes of the other country. India and Bangladesh have also maintained an agreement namely the "Protocol on Inland Water Transit and Trade" to facilitate bilateral trade and commerce through the use of cross-border inland waterways. The existing protocol was renewed on 24th March, 2009 and it will be valid upto 31st March 2012.

The salient features of the Protocol are given below. The detailed protocol is attached as Annex 3.

- Carriage of cargo of inter-country trade/cross-border trade.
- Carriage of cargo between two places of one country through the territory of the other. Mainly transporting cargo between Kolkata and IWT stations in Assam (Pandu and Karimganj) and between Pandu and Karimganj.
- Each country shall ensure smooth navigation in the routes within its geographical jurisdiction and will extend necessary navigational facilities. Night navigation is allowed where such facilities exist.
- Vessels must be registered under the prevailing act of either country (Inland Shipping Ordinance, 1976 in case of Bangladesh vessels, Inland Vessels Act, 1917 in case of Indian vessels).
- Vessels operating under the protocol will take specific routes according to the following:

  i. Kolkata – Chandpur – Mawa – Sirajganj – Pandu – Silghat and reverse

  ii. Kolkata – Chandpur – Ashuganj – Sherpur – Zakiganj – Karimganj and reverse

  iii. Silghat – Pandu – Sirajganj – Mawa – Ashuganj – Sherpur – Zakiganj Karimgaanj and reverse

  iv. Rajshahi – Godagari – Dhulian and reverse

A total of 10 ports of call, 5 on each side are designated for loading/unloading of inter-country trade cargo. These are presented in Table 4.2,

Table 4.2

List of Ports of Call in Bangladesh and India

	Bangladesh	*India*
1	Narayanganj	Kolkata
2	Mongla	Haldia
3	Khukna	Karimganj
4	Sirajganj	Pandu
5	Ashuganj	Silghat

- The vessels of either country while plying in the water of the other country shall be permitted to purchase fuels and essential stores at places mentioned in the Protocol. Night halt points have also been specified in the Protocol.
- The vessels intended to operate under the Protocol will obtain permission of the competent authorities appointed by the respective governments. The Bangladesh Inland Water Transport Authority (BIWTA) in Bangladesh and the Inland Waterways Authority of India (IWAI) in India have been appointed as competent authorities responsible for all work under the protocol by their respective governments.
- The operators of both the countries will charge to the extent of practicable uniform freight rates for the carriage of both inter-country trade cargo and transit cargo.
- The vessel of one country while plying in the waters of the other

country shall fly its national flag along with the national flag of the other country.

- The competent authorities of one country shall provide all necessary assistance to the vessel of the other country if it is grounded, capsized or otherwise in distress.
- If a vessel while plying in the other country is in trouble, it will be allowed to go to the dockyard along the route.
- All vessels will have to pay conservancy, berthing, landing and shipping charges, canal charges, etc. This will be charged at a rate at par with local vessels.
- Pilotage services will be provided to the vessels of the other country on preferential basis.
- Vessels in transit are not allowed to carry goods for inter-country trade, carriage of domestic cargo or passenger while in operation under the Protocol.
- Vessels are required to keep all necessary documents on board and are liable for showing them to any appropriate authority.
- Customer services are provided at all "Ports of Call" or other extended places in accordance with the prevailing rules and procedures.
- The stretches between Sirajganj and Daikhawa in the river Brahmaputra and between Sherpur and Zakiganj in the river Kushiyara are identified as routes primarily maintained for Indian transit traffic. The Government of India pays an agreed amount towards the conservancy cost of these routes. Presently this amount is 55 million BD Taka annually (Stakeholder consultation, Mr Syed Monwar Hossain, 2011).
- Bangladesh trucks may carry cargo trans-shipped from vessels at Ashuganj and Sherpur to the Indian border

4.4 Critical Points Constraining the Development

The bilateral protocol envisages a mutually beneficial arrangement for the use of waterways for facilitating trade and commerce between the countries and for passage of goods between two places of one country through the territory of the other. However, certain provisions of the Protocol itself are not conducive and corollary to the spirit of the Protocol. Some provisions which are considered to be hindrances to facilitating the inland navigation trade between the countries are described below.

a. Night Navigation Facilities

Round the clock operation of vessels not only increases the turn round but also capacity utilisation. Substantial reduction of transportation time could also make inland navigation more vibrant and competitive to other modes as well. However, the Protocol unfortunately does not provide for mandatory provision of installing night navigation facilities all the way in the protocol routes. Article 2.1 states that night navigation is allowed where such facilities already exist. More than two-third of the protocol routes presently do not have night navigation facilities. On these long routes, vessels can only operate 12 hours a day and increases the transportation time.

b. Ports of Call

According to Article 11 of the Protocol some places of the respective countries are nominated as 'Ports of Call' (Table 4.2).

According to this provision vessels engaged in inter-country trade are allowed to load/ unload only at the nominated 'Port of Call'. If the cargo from Kolkata in India is destined for Barisal or Chandpur in Bangladesh, the vessel will have to run to Narayanganj and after customs formalities the vessel will have to come back again to the destination. This is contrary to the scenario prevailing in road transport. Cargo destined for any place in Bangladesh comes to Benapole or to any road based land port and after customs formalities starts its journey to the destination. As such cross-border trade by inland navigation loses its competitiveness to the roads. This is because the 'Ports of Call' are far away from the entry/exit points. There are the following three pairs of entry/

exit points in the Indo-Bangla Protocol routes:

	Bangladesh	*India*
1	Angtihara	Namkhana
2	Daikhawa	Dhubri
3	Zakiganj	Karimganj

The first two pairs are not full-fledged custom stations, but only provide customs checking. Full-fledged customs formalities are provided only at designated 'Ports of Call' although the Article 21 states that both the countries agree to have customs stations at or near the points of entry and exit in each country.

c. Extension of Protocol Routes

The term 'route' in the Protocol refers to eight certain routes determined in the Article 1.2. Vessels are not allowed to go beyond the route even if there exists transport demand. In such cases transportation by other modes are inevitable and trans-shipment increase the transportation time and cost.

d. Utilisation of Vessels in the Domestic Transport of Other Country

Being one of the largest IWT nations, Bangladesh has a large IWT fleet numbering more than 3000 cargo vessels with a static capacity of 1.23 million tonne. Almost all movement takes place (other than POL movement from Assam) by Bangladesh barges as they have the following advantages:

- Higher draft (3.5 m to 4.0 m) and higher fuel efficiency.
- Cost of manning is low compared to their Indian counterparts.
- Cost of fuel in Bangladesh is cheaper by approximately ₹ 10/- per litre.
- Cost of construction is lower than that in India.

These advantages are to be fully exploited to expand trade and cargo volumes. The capacity of Bangladesh vessels are not utilised to the full extent. Bangladesh vessels may contribute substantially in the carriage of goods in domestic routes of India. Article 17 of the Protocol prohibits such operation.

4.5 Potentiality of Traffic in the River Kushiyara

A preliminary study conducted in 2006 by the Inland Waterways Authority of India (IWAI) estimated that the total volume of freight movement between mainland India and north-eastern states was 20 million tonne annually. The study concluded that if trans-shipment is allowed at Ashuganj and if the route between Ashuganj and Karimganj be developed for perennial navigation, one-third of the total volume might be diverted to the rivers. The IWAI estimated an annual traffic of 6 million tonne of which 1.5 million tonne will move in the Kolkata-Karimganj route.

Karimganj is an important distribution/consolidation centre to and from different destinations in lower Assam, Meghalaya and Manipur. Traffic demand is growing due to economic growth in the hinterland of Karimganj. It may be mentioned here that the route between Kolkata and Karimganj will be further extended involving the river Barak. The IWAI has already proposed to declare Bhanga (upstream of Karimganj) to Lakhipur via the Silchar route (121 km) as a national waterway. The total development cost of this route was estimated by the IWAI at ₹ 46 crore. With the development and opening of this route freight movement by river will be further extended to the interior places of the north-east. Silchar is an important multi-modal hub in the north-east involving rail and road. As a result of the extension of inland navigation upto Silchar, traffic demand will be further increased. The Ashuganj-Karimganj stretch, being in between the proposed National Waterway above Karimganj and the deeper river portion below Ashuganj in the transit route to Kolkata and Silghat, will determine the overall navigability in the GBM-Barak

IWT system and hence its development for round the year navigation is crucial for sustainable IWT operations. Extension of the Indo-Bangla Protocol route to Silchar will not only ensure expeditious movement of transit cargo, it will also promote export trade at the same time from Bangladesh to the north-east.

5

Geo-morphological Setting and Historical Changes

5.1 Geological Setting

The Kalni-Kushiyara River is one of the major rivers in the northeast region of Bangladesh. This river system constitutes the subsiding Sylhet Trough which is a sub-basin of the Bengal Basin. The southern and eastern parts of the Sylhet Trough are characterised by a series of north trending folds which have formed as a result of deformation from the Indo-Burman ranges. This region experiences some of the greatest subsidence. But there is no common consensus regarding the rate of subsidence among geologists. The subsidence rate was mentioned as 2 cm/y according to Morgan and McIntire (1959). FAP 6 study (SNC *et al.*, 1998c) also collected a few peat samples from the Sylhet Basin and estimated the age of deposition through carbon dating. They have found that the subsidence is about 1 mm/year, which is 20 times much smaller than Morgan and McIntire's estimation. The maximum isostatic subsidence rate of the Sylhet Basin close to at the northern boundary would be 3 mm/year as indicated by Goodbred and Kuehl (2000) and subsidence for the compaction can be assumed to be an additional 1 to 2 mm/year.

5.2 Delineating the Sylhet Basin

CEGIS (2011) delineated the Sylhet Basin based on their topographical characteristics (Figure 5.1). It is a tub-shaped Basin, more than 100 km long at its north-south axis. The east-west cross profile of the Basin shows a very high topographical slope, 15 to 25 cm/km with a 40 to 50 km wide flat bottom (Figure 5.2). The figure shows that the levees of the river are 2 to 3 m higher than the flood basins. The Sylhet Basin is dissected by the levees of the present and previous courses of many rivers like the Surma, the Kuhsiyara, the Baulaii and the Mogra.

Long-profile of the Sylhet Basin (Figure 5.3) shows that the Basin bottom in the northern part is about 2 m lower than the southern boundary where there is an outlet of the Basin. All the rivers from east and west enter into the Basin flowing in the west and east direction respectively over the side slopes. These rivers then turn to the south and flow into the outlet through the Meghna River. Although the topography showed a negative slope, the gradient of the river levees are in line with the drainage direction.

The observed reverse slope along the axis of the Basin is mainly due to a differential subsidence rate, which is higher in the northern part. For thousands of years, the Brahmaputra River had been feeding sediment to the subsiding Sylhet Basin. Avulsion of the river from the southwest boundary of the Basin to its present course cut the main sediment source of the Basin, which created a negative balance between sedimentation and subsidence in the Sylhet Basin. However, the differential net subsidence of the Basin has greatly influenced the changes in the river courses (Goodbred and Kuehl, 2000).

5.3 Changes in Course of the Kushiyara during the Previous Centuries

During the last 240 years, the Kushiyara River has changed its course several times. The location of bifurcation of the river from the Barak was at the same location as at present. At that time after flowing 15 km along the present course of the Kushiyara, the river flowed 40 km along the present course of the Sonai Bardal River. The present course of the Sonai Bardal seems to be the old course of the Kushiyara River. At the immediate downstream of the confluence with the Manu River, the course of the Kushiyara was different from the present course. The river used to flow along a course which was south of Nabiganj upazila sadar and close to Habigang town. The river met with the flow of the Surma River a few kilometers upstream of the Lakhai.

The map of 1840 (Tassin's map) indicates that the upstream reach of the river shifted from the course of the Sonai Bardal to the present course of the Kushiyara River. The course of the rest of the river was similar to that shown in Rennel's map. The map of early 1920 shows a major avulsion of the course of the Kushiyara River. At the immediate downstream of the Manu confluence, the Kushiyara occupied the course of the smaller distributaries of the Surma and local drainage channel and met with the Mora Surma (Kalni River) close to Markuli. Downstream of Markuli, the river is known as the Kalni-Kushiyara River. This course flowed close to Ajmiriganj, occupying the previous course of the Surma. By this

Figure 5.1

DEM shows the Boundary of Sylhet Basin and its Bottom

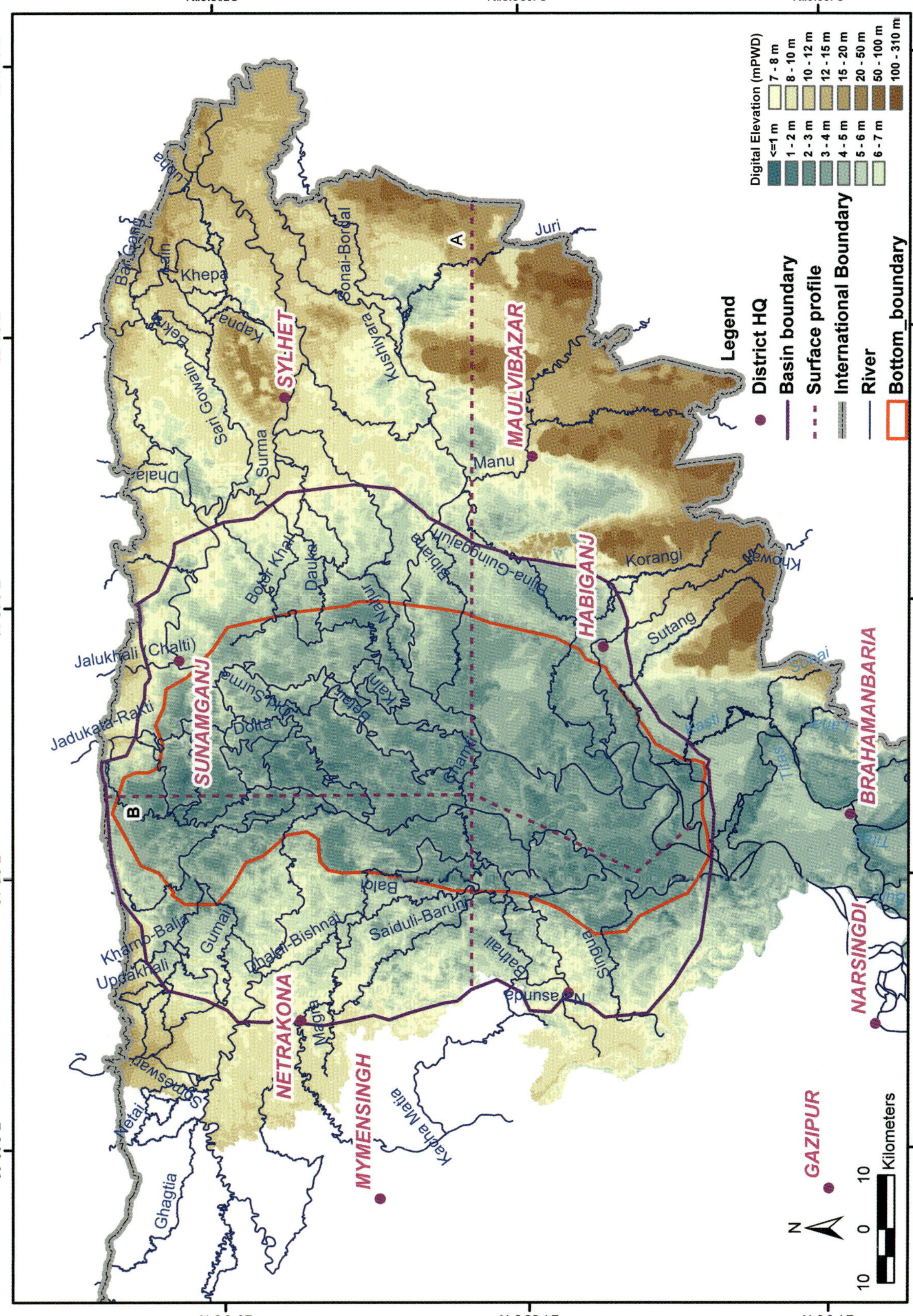

Source: CEGIS, 2011a.

Figure 5.2

Cross Profile of Sylhet Basin (Along line A of Figure 5.1)

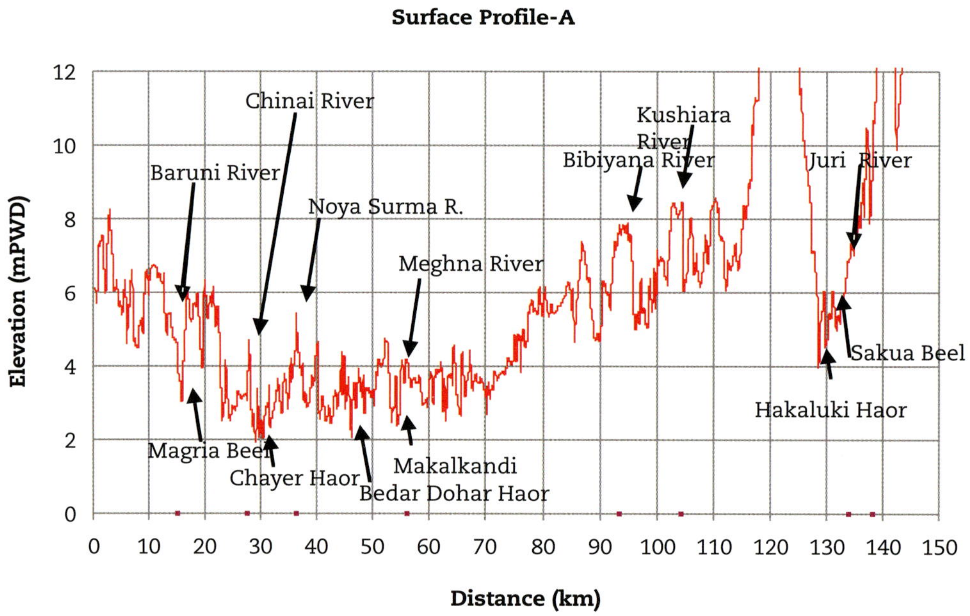

Source: CEGIS, 2011a.

Figure 5.3

Long Profile of Sylhet Basin (Along line B of Figure 5.1)

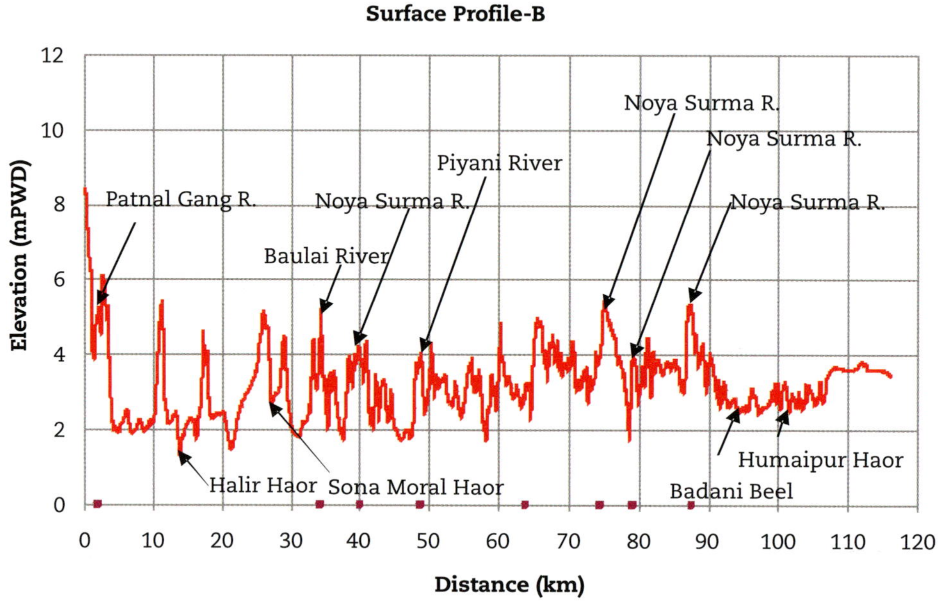

Source: CEGIS, 2011a.

Figure 5.4

Changes in the Course of the Kushiyara River Over Time

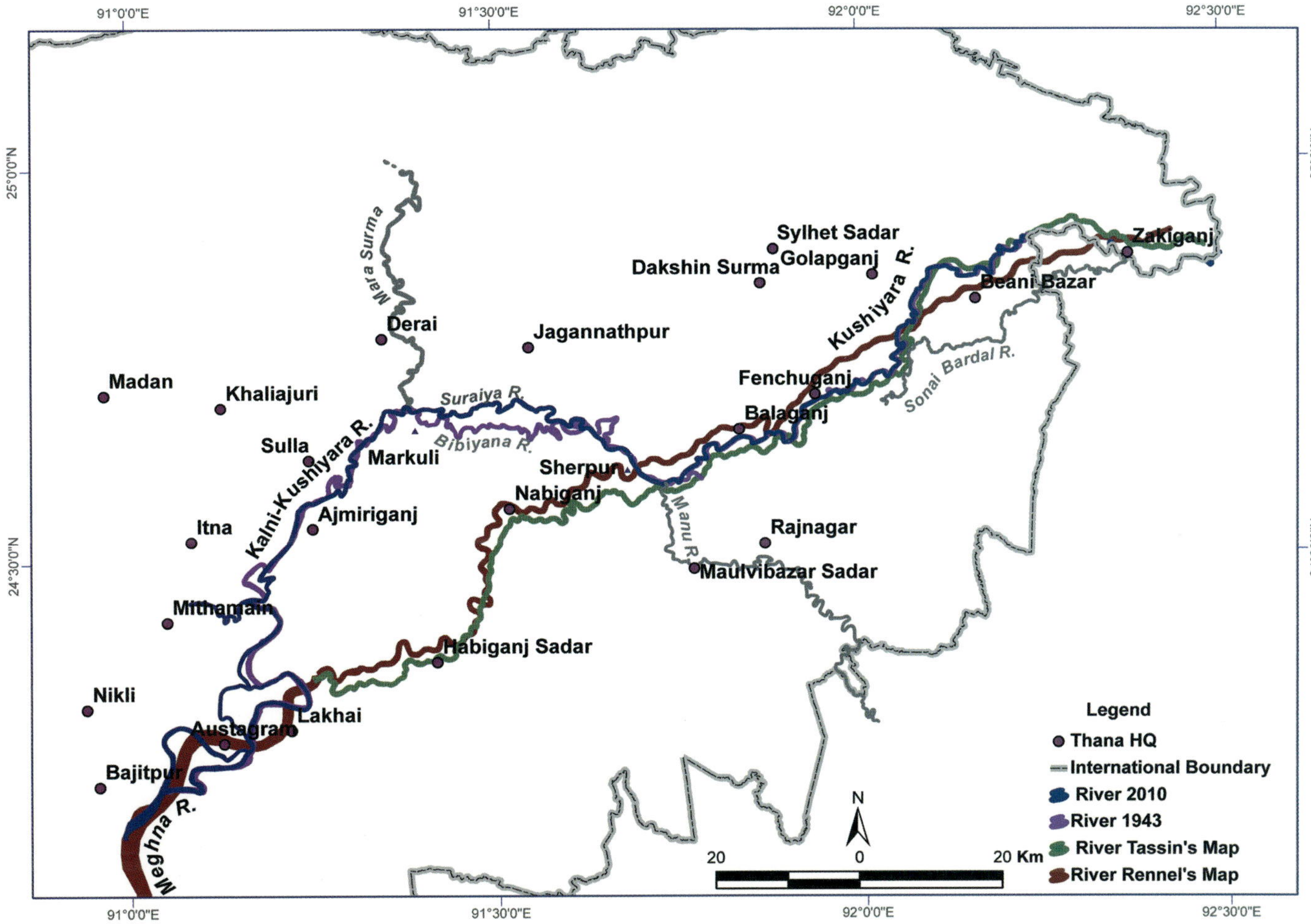

Source: CEGIS, 2011a.

time the main flow of the Surma occupied its present course.

The present course of the Kushiyara River was almost similar to that of early last century. There was only one avulsion through the course of the Bibiyana River downstream of Shepur Bridge. The length of the avulsion course was about 25 km and only a few kilometers north of the previous course (Figure 5.4).

5.4 Role of the Subsidence in Changing the River Courses

According to Schumm *et al.* (2000), and Burnett and Schumm (1983) subsidence or uplift due to tectonic activities has pronounced effects on the shifting process of river courses and morphology. The subsidence and uplifting often causes the avulsion of rivers, changes their planform pattern from braided to sinuosity or the other way around, and increases or decreases sinuosity. Different studies reveal that there is net subsidence in the Sylhet Basin, which is at a higher rate at the northern part of the Basin. The estimated rate of maximum subsidence was about a meter during the last 200 years after avulsion of the Brahmaputra River (CEGIS, 2011). The shifting of the courses of the Kushiyara, Surma, and Someswari and Kangsha rivers in the last 240 years followed a particular direction, towards the north, where the rate of subsidence was maximum (Figure 5.5).

These rivers shifted their courses from an upper to a lower level-from south to the

Figure 5.5

Recent Changes in the Surma-Kushiyara River Courses

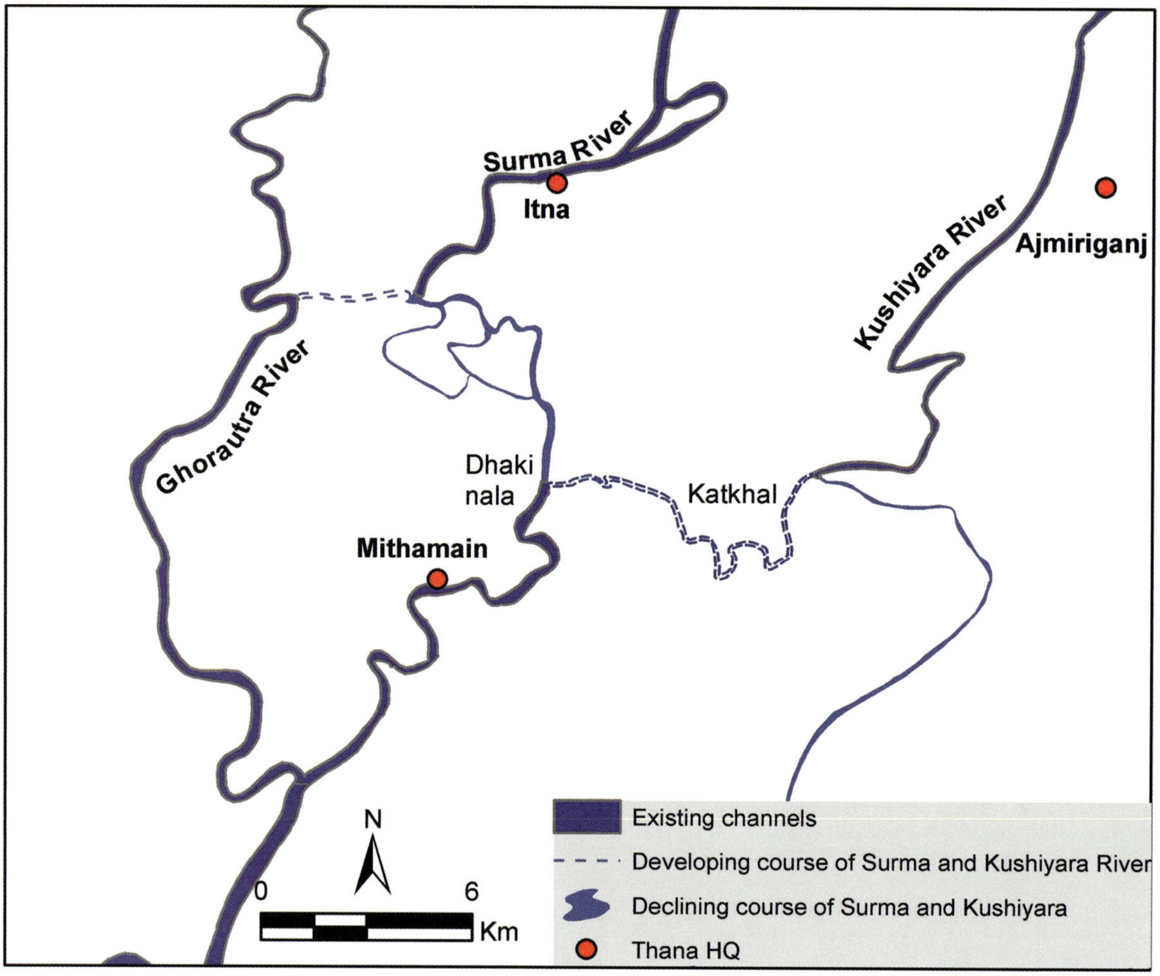

Source: CEGIS, 2011a.

north, while the ultimate flow direction of these rivers were north to south at the bottom of the Sylhet Basin. The process of the development of the rivers after their courses shifted where the topography is reverse to the direction of the flow is described in Chapter 7.

5.5 Recent Avulsions in the Surma-Kushiyara System

Changes of the river courses in the northeast region are not only occurring in the century scale, but also in the decade scale. Two such changes as in Figure 5.5 are identified using recent satellite images. One of these changes has occurred in the Kushiyara River downstream of Ajmiriganj. Time series satellite images of 24 to 30 m resolution do not show any such changes having occurred in the early 1990s. However, the image of Landsat image 1997 shows the existence of a narrow channel linking the Kushiyara River with the Surma River. The process of this change was recognised by FAP 6 (SNC *et al.*, 1998a) in the late 1990s. Satellite images of 2010 shows that the Kushiyara River downstream of Katkhal has dried up completely. The Hydrographic Survey Chart of 2010 prepared by the BIWTA also shows huge sedimentation in the Kushiyara River downstream of the off-take of the new channel. This new channel takes-off from its parent river following the same alignment as at the upstream. On the other hand, the downstream reach of the Kushiyara has made a 'U' turn, more than 300^{0} with its upstream reach. This high deviation angle at the bifurcation was probably the cause of the decline of the main channel and helped in the development of the new channel. At present a new narrow channel has been diverting all the dry season flow to the Surma River at Dhaki at the immediate upstream of Mithamain, as shown in Figure 5.5. This avulsion has significant effects on the navigability of the Kushiyara River.

The diversion of flow of the Kushiyara River caused to raise the water level in the Surma River, which may have triggered the development of a new diversion channel from this river further west to the Ghorautra River. The process of development of these two channels was almost simultaneous. The development of these two channels appears to be the result of the two individual but related events of local morphology. Although not substantiated by data, the intrinsic cause might also be the topographical changes that occurred in the last decades by sediment input from the Kushiyara River.

6

Hydro-morphological Characteristics of the Kushiyara River

6.1 General

Since the Barak River flow became divided, the Kushiyara has been carrying a larger share of flow of its parent river. There are a number of tributaries that meet at the downstream with the Kushsiyara. Among these tributaries, the contribution of the Manu River in terms of dry and monsoon discharge is significant. The hydro-morphological characteristics of the river such as discharge, water levels at different gauging stations in the Kushiyara River, sediment transport, bed material characteristics, width, riverbank erosion, breaching of levees, and cut-off process are discussed in the following sections.

Figure 6.1

Discharge Hydrograph of the Kushiyara at Sheola (Analysis was Conducted by CEGIS at October, 2011)

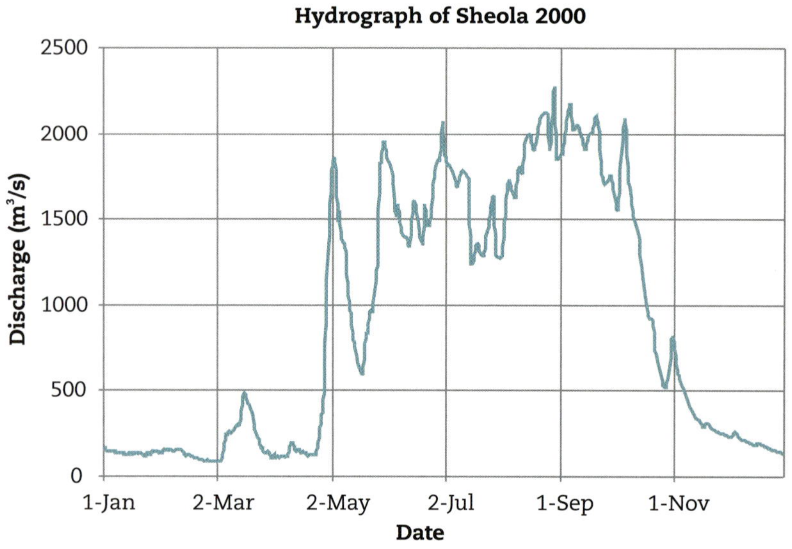

Figure 6.2

Date-wise Maximum and Minimum Flow in the Kushiyara River at Sheola (Analysis was Conducted by CEGIS at October, 2011)

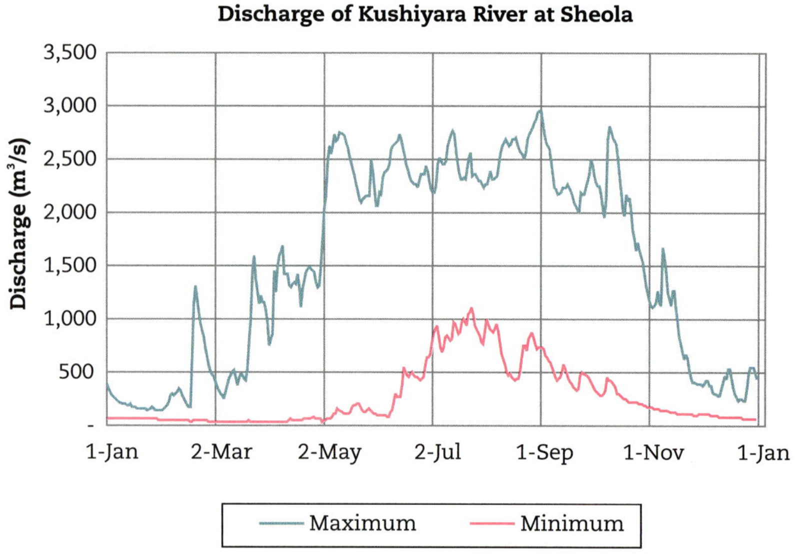

6.2 Discharge

There are two discharge gauging stations of the BWDB (Figure 6.1) in the Kushiyara River at Sheola and Sherpur and one gauging station in the Manu River at the Manu Railway Bridge. A typical discharge hydrograph of the Kushiyara River at Sheola for the year 2000 is presented in Figure 6.1. From January to April the discharge was below 200 m^3/s with a small increase and subsequent decrease in February. It suddenly increased at the end of April and reached the value of 1800 m^3/s within a few days. The figure shows a broad peak from May to mid-October. Plotting of date-wise maximum and minimum discharges from 1964 to 2006 also shows a very wide range of time for the occurrence of high discharges. The limit is varied from early May to mid-October (Figure 6.2). During this period the date-wise variation of discharge was very high from 200 m^3/s to 3,000 m^3/s. The average annual flood discharge in the Kushiyara River at Sheola was about 2,500 m^3/s (Figure 6.2). Annual maximum discharge was low at about 1700 m^3/s in the 1960s and in the mid 1980s it increased to 3,000 m^3/s but after that the maxium flood dishchage reduced to 2,000 m^3/s in the recent past. No significant trend has been observed except for the decade-scale variation during the last four decades (Figure 6.3). Annual minimum discharge shows a slight increasing trend up to 1993 and the value reaches 100 m^3/s while it was about 50 m^3/s during 1965 (Analysis was conducted By CEGIS in October, 2011).

During monsoon, the maximum contirbution of the Manu River to the Kushsiyara was about 600 m^3/s and dry season minimum contribution was about 8 m^3/s. There is almost no trend over the period.

Figure 6.3

Variation of Annual Maximum and Minimum Flow in the Kushiyara River at Sheola (Analysis was Conducted by CEGIS at October, 2011)

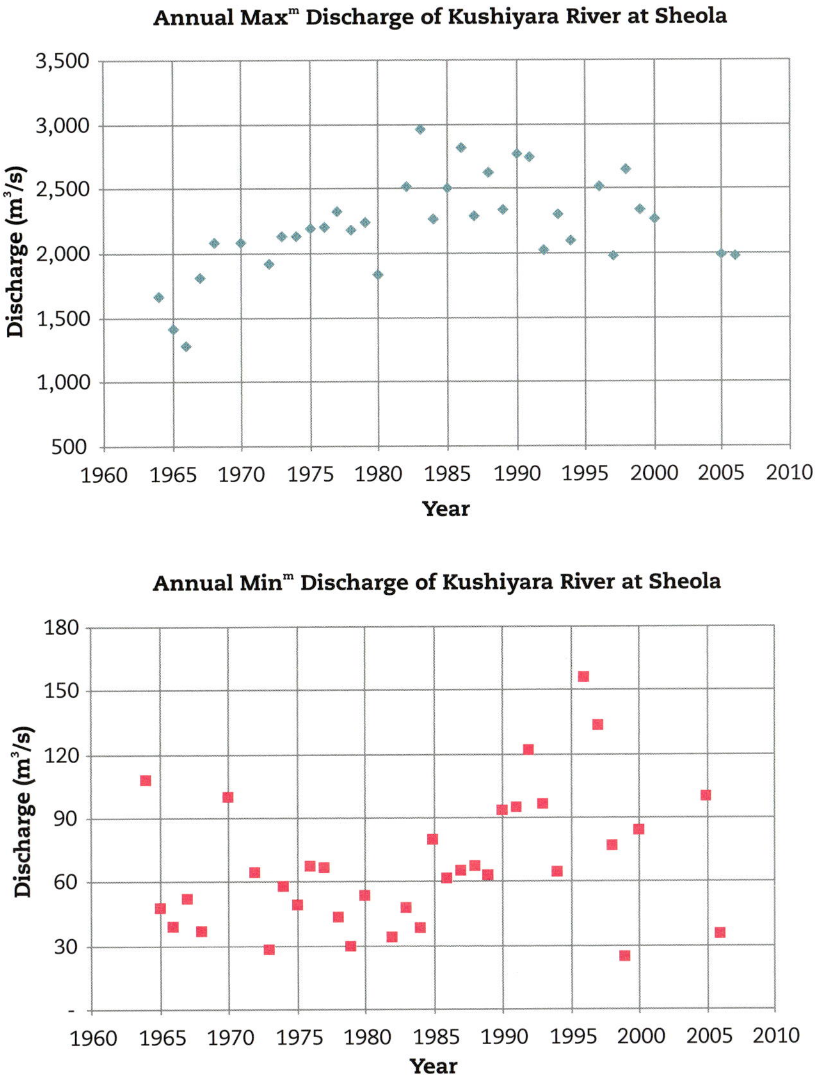

6.3 Water Level

The dry season water level of the lower reach (up to Markuli) of the Kushiyara River is influenced by tide. The daily variation during dry season is a few centimeters. However, upstream of Markuli no tidal influence has been observed. Frequency hydrographs of water level at Sheola representating the upstream reaches and at Ajmirigani representating downstream reaches are presented to show the range of yearly variation in water level at different rates. Moreover, annual minimum water levels at different gauging stations are presented and compared in the following paragraphs.

6.3.1 Water Level at Sheola

From frequency hydrograph analysis which shows the 90 per cent probability of excidence of water level, the range of variation of water level at Sheola has been more than 10 meter varying from a minimum of 4 mPWD to a maximum of 14 mPWD over the last 40 years. Water level at a particular date may also vary over the years and such variation may exceed a maximum of 10 meter during April and May

Figure 6.4

Variation of Annual Maximum and Minimum Flow in the Manu River at Manu Railway Bridge (Analysis was conducted by CEGIS at October, 2011)

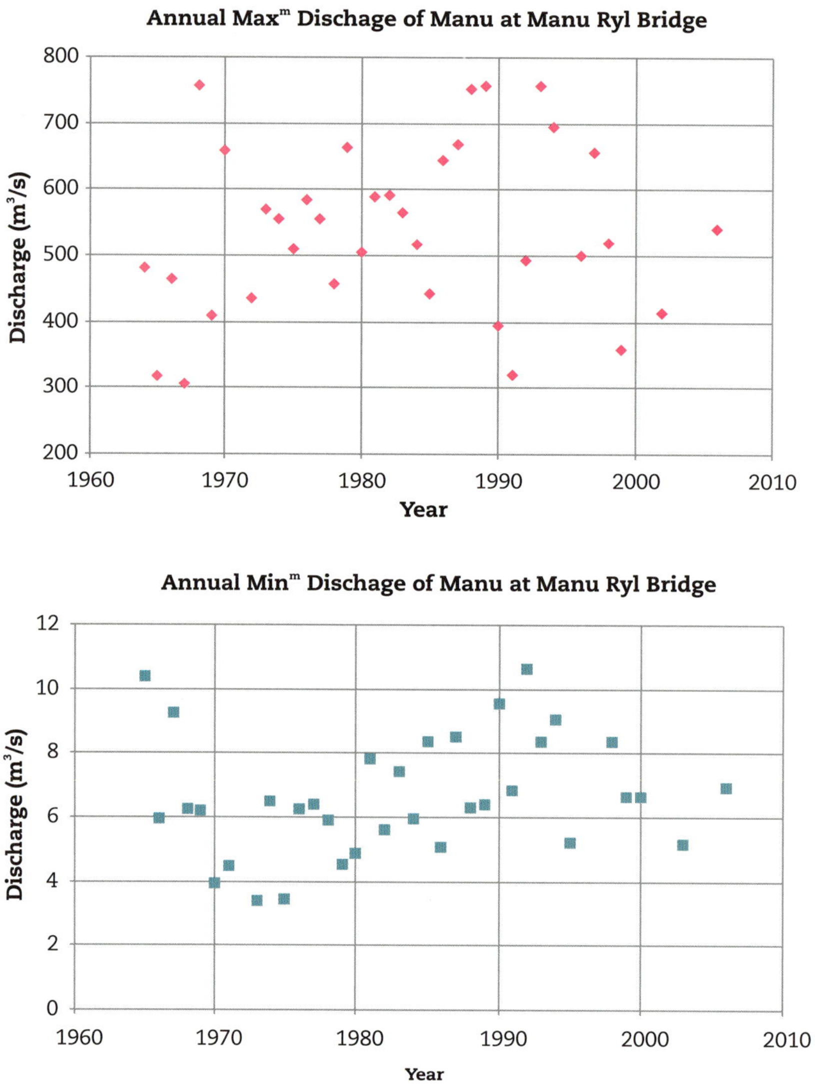

(Figure 6.5). The range of date-wise variation in water level reduces from November and continues up to the end of February. During monsoon, especially July and August, this range is also low.

At Sheola the annual maximum water level from 1950 shows a slight increasing trend from 13.5 mPWD to 14.2 mPWD (Figure 6.5). Increase in discharge from the mid 1960s might be one of the reasons for the observed increase of water level. However, the water level during the last two decades have not shown any decrease in annual maximum discharge. The annual minimum water level remains nearly unchanged, the average value of which is 4.3 mPWD (Analysis was conducted By CEGIS in October, 2011).

6.3.2 Water Level at Ajmiriganj

Historical records from 1964 to 2008 show that the water level of the Kushiyara River may vary from 1 to 8.5 mPWD at Ajmiriganj (Figure 6.7). Water level at a particular date may vary in a wide range from year to year. This range of variation is high from December to May, which differs

Figure 6.5

Frequency Hydrograph of Water Level at Sheola (Analysis was conducted by CEGIS at October, 2011)

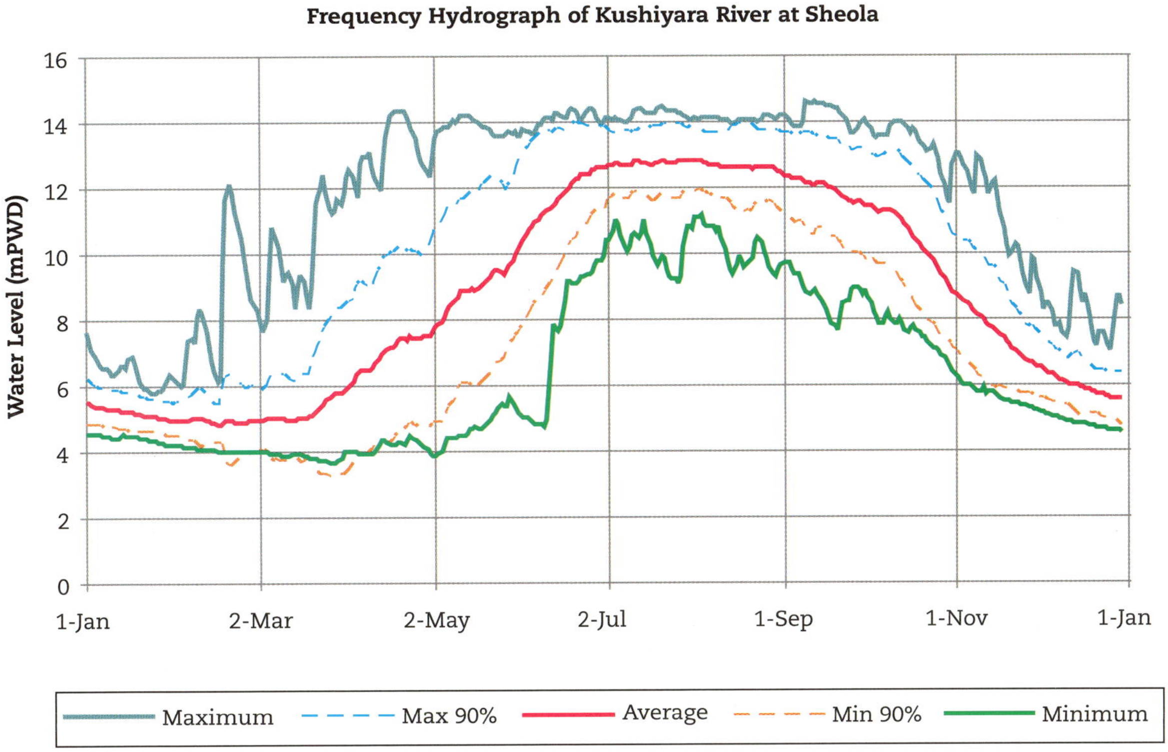

Figure 6.6

Annual Maximum and Minimum Water Level at Sheola (Analysis was conducted by CEGIS at October, 2011)

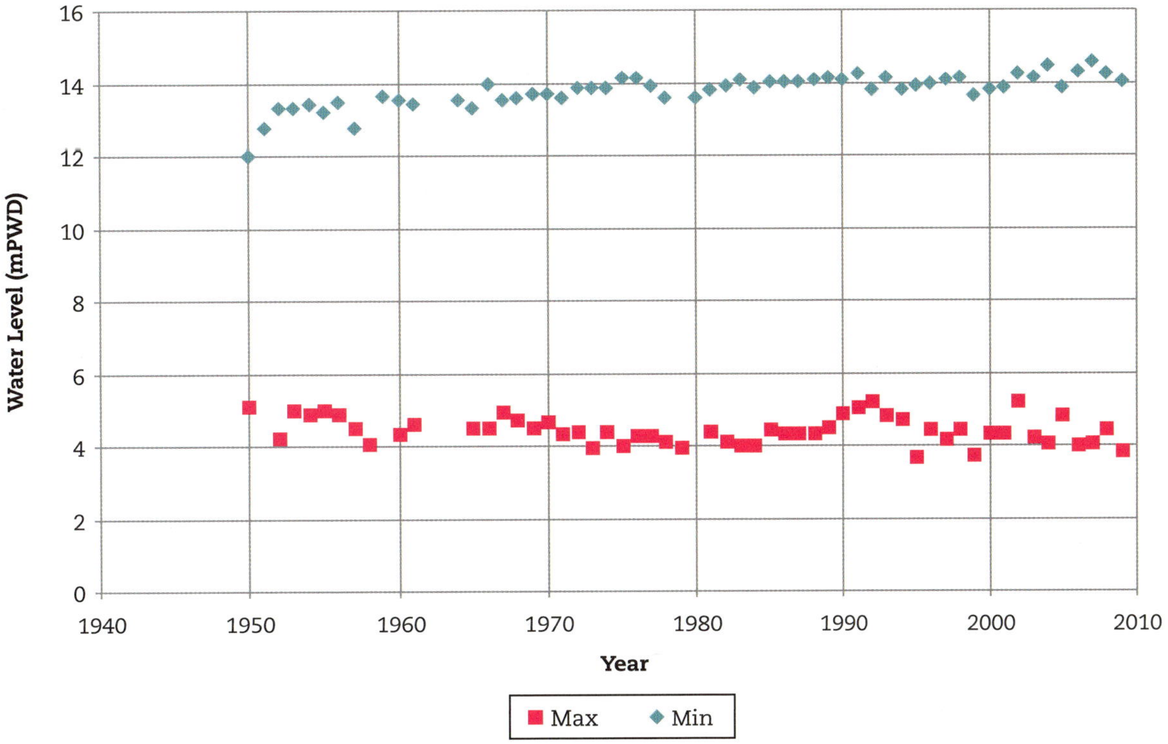

Figure 6.7

Frequency Hydrograph of Water Level at Ajmiriganj (Analysis was conducted by CEGIS at October, 2011)

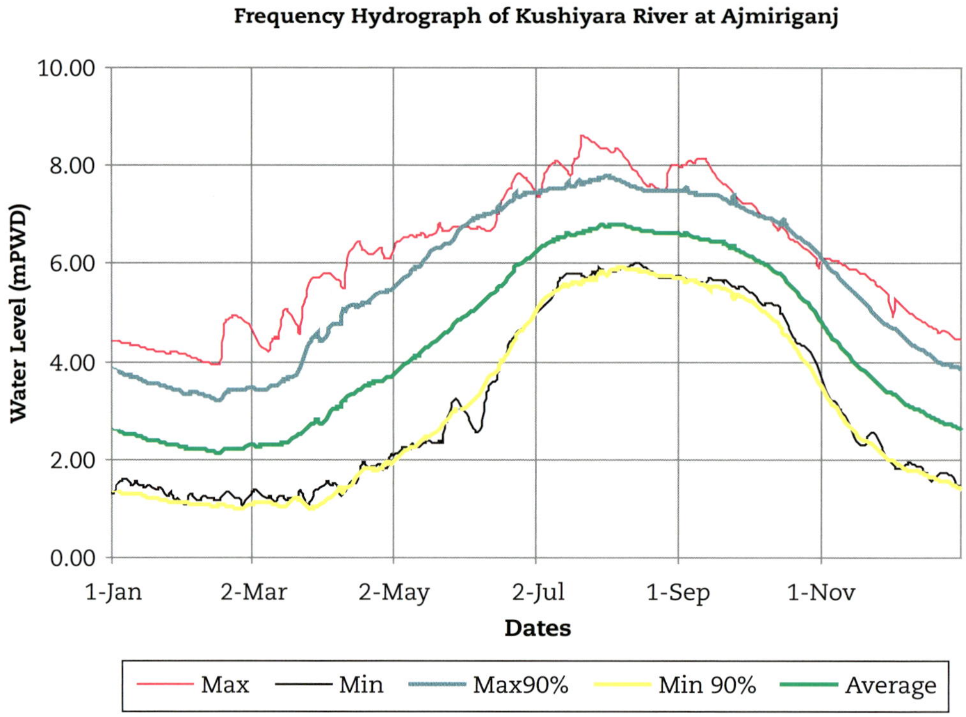

Figure 6.8

Annual Maximum and Minimum Water Level at Ajmiriganj (Analysis was conducted by CEGIS at October, 2011)

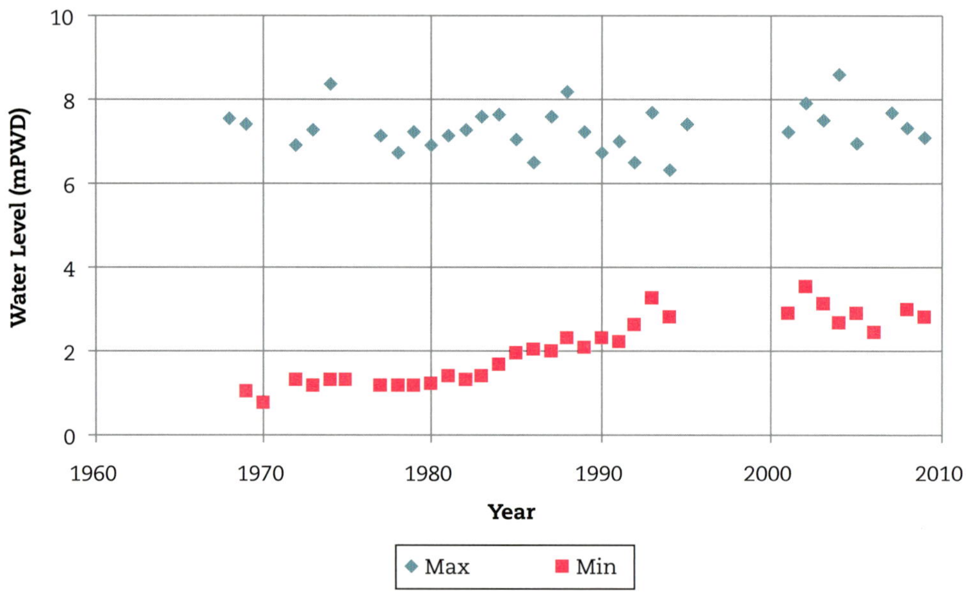

slightly from that of Sheola. Like Sheola, uncertainty in the water level reduces during thc monsoon.

Annual maximum and minimum water levels show almost no variation in maximum water level, but there was a very significant rise of minimum water level from the mid 1980s (Figure 6.8). The rise in minimum water level reached its maximum value in the mid 1990s and started to come down recently (shown in Figure 6.8).

During the dry period maximum tidal range was about 0.2 m during the mid 1980s but afterwards it reduced to only 0.05 m (Figure 6.9). This reduction is in phase with the rising of annual minimum water level. The reduction in tidal range and simultaneous rising of annual minimum water level indicate a disturbance in the river regime downstream of Ajmiriganj (Analysis was conducted By CEGIS in October, 2011).

6.3.3 Changes in Annual Minimum Water Level in the Kushiyara River

Annual maximum water levels along the Kushisyara River have not shown any significant trend over time during the last five decades. However, annual minimum water levels at Ajmiriganj and its upstream at Markuli are found to increase significantly from the mid 1980s (Figure 6.10). No such changes are observed in the downstream gauging station at Madna. These observations suggest that there have been changes in the river morphology between Ajmiriganj and Madna since the mid 1980s, the effects of which are continuing till date.

6.4 Sediment

There was only one sediment gauging station of the BWDB along the Kushiyara River at Sheola. There were sediment gauging stations in the rivers coming from Tripura Hills such as the Manu, Khowai and Dhalai rivers, which feed the Kushiyara River at the downstream of Sheola. FAP 6 used the sediment concentration and bed material data from the BWDB and the Surface Water Modeling Centre (SWMC) including the primary data that they had collected themselves. The result presented in this section is mainly based on the FAP 6 report (SNC *et al.*, 1997)

CEGIS also carried out a sediment sampling campaign in September 2011 in the downstream reach of the Kushiyara River. It measured flow velocity, sediment concentration and bed material samples

Figure 6.9

Variation of Tidal Range in the Months of January, February and March (Analysis was conducted by CEGIS at October, 2011)

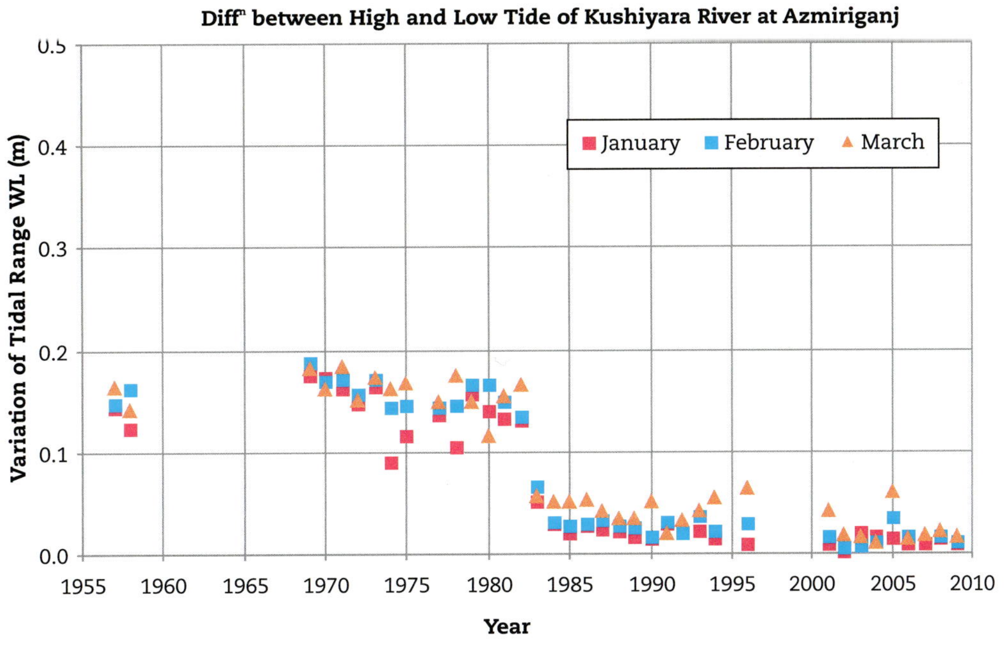

Figure 6.10

Annual Minimum Water Level at Different Stations of Kushiyara (Analysis was conducted by CEGIS at October, 2011)

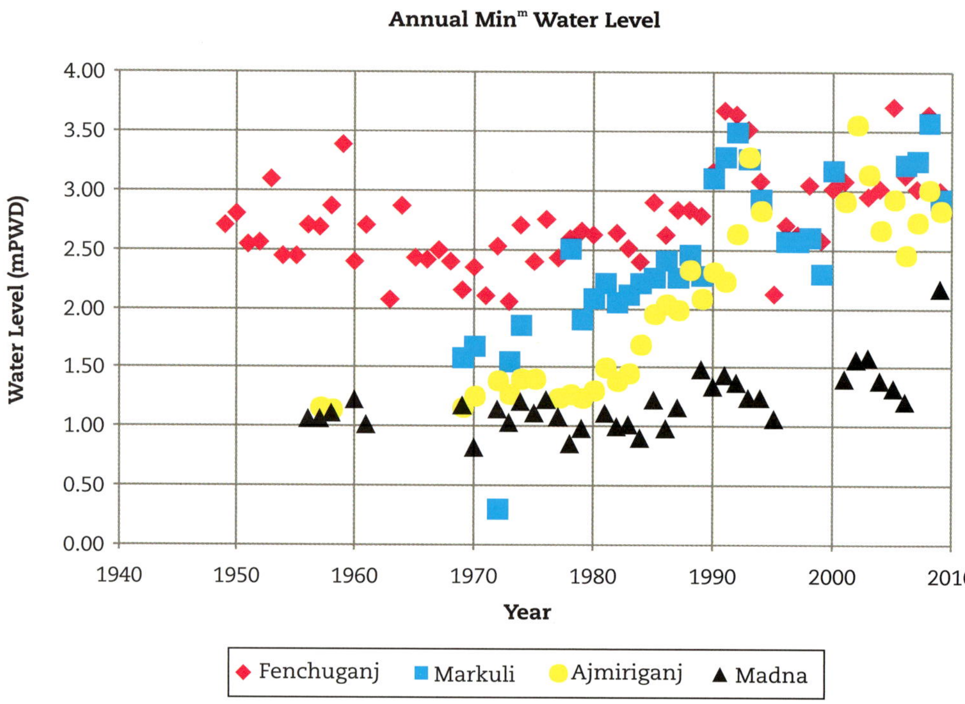

along the Dhaki Nala (a new developing course of the Kushiyara River) and the Kushiyara River from Khatkhal to Shepur (Figure 6.11). The result is also presented in the following paragraphs.

6.4.1 Kushiyara River at Sheola

The average suspended sediment concentration in the Kushiyara River at Sheola was found to be 253 mg/l and ranged between 4 mg/l and 4,639 mg/l. Daily suspended load of this river ranged between 22 tonne/day and 427,600 tonne/day. The average annual suspended sediment load was found to be 8.6 million tonne/year which ranged between 4.2 and 15.8 million tonne/year. Seasonal distribution of the load was estimated to be 4 per cent at pre-monsoon, 80 per cent at monsoon, 11 per cent at post-monsoon and 1 per cent at dry season. The suspended sediment of this river consisted of 20 per cent sand, 54 per cent silt and 24 per cent clay. Bed material samples at that station indicated that the D_{50} and D_{10} sizes were around 0.1 mm and 0.06 mm respectively. The annual sand load (bed material load) was estimated to be 2 million tonne/year.

6.4.2 Tripura Hills Streams

The Manu, Dhalai and Khowai rivers of Tripura Hills Streams were taken for this sediment analysis. Data were collected from the rail crossing by the Manu River, from Kamalganj by the Dhalai River and from Shaistaganj by the Khowai River. Among the rivers of this region, these sites recorded the highest suspended sediment concentrations. The suspended sediment concentrations were estimated to be up to 9300 mg/l in the Dhalai River and up to 7665 mg/l in the Manu River. The average observed concentration exceeded 1000 mg/l in the Dhalai River, 799 mg/l in the Manu River and 608 mg/l in the Khowai River. The composition of suspended sediment was collected from the station at the Khowai River. The suspended sediment of this river consisted of 33 per cent sand, 49 per cent silt and 18 per cent clay. The bed material size indicated that D_{10} size was around 0.06 mm. The seasonal distribution of the annual average sediment load was found to be 10 per cent at pre-monsoon, 80 per cent at monsoon, 9 per cent at post-monsoon and 1 per cent at dry season.

Figure 6.11

Locations of Sediment Sampling in the Kushiyara River (Measured by CEGIS at September 2011)

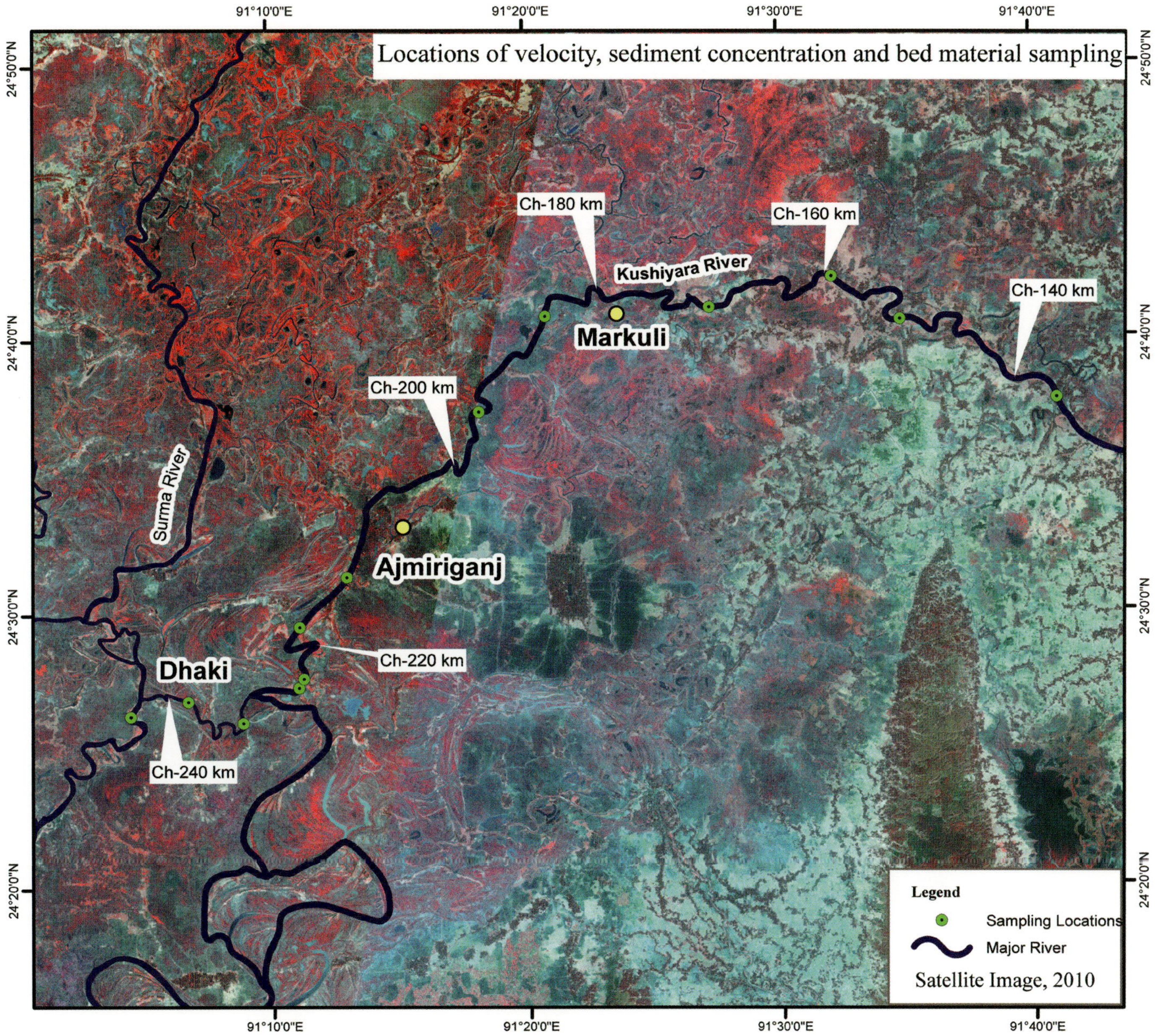

The annual suspended sediment loads have been estimated as follows:

Manu River: average load = 4.9 million tonne/year (range 1.4-10.4 million tonne/year)

Dhalai River: average load = 1.6 million tonne/year (range 1.6-2.5 million tonne/year)

Khowai River: average load = 1.7 million tonne/year (range 0.2-6.0 million tonne/year)

6.4.3 Sediment Sampling

Sediment measured at mid-depth of each vertical and average concentration was found to be 600 mg/l, with minimum and maximum sediment concentrations of 400 to 1400 mg/l respectively up to Ajmiriganj.

Figure 6.12

Surface Velocity, Sediment Concentration and Bed Materials along the Kushiyara River (Measured by CEGIS at September 2011)

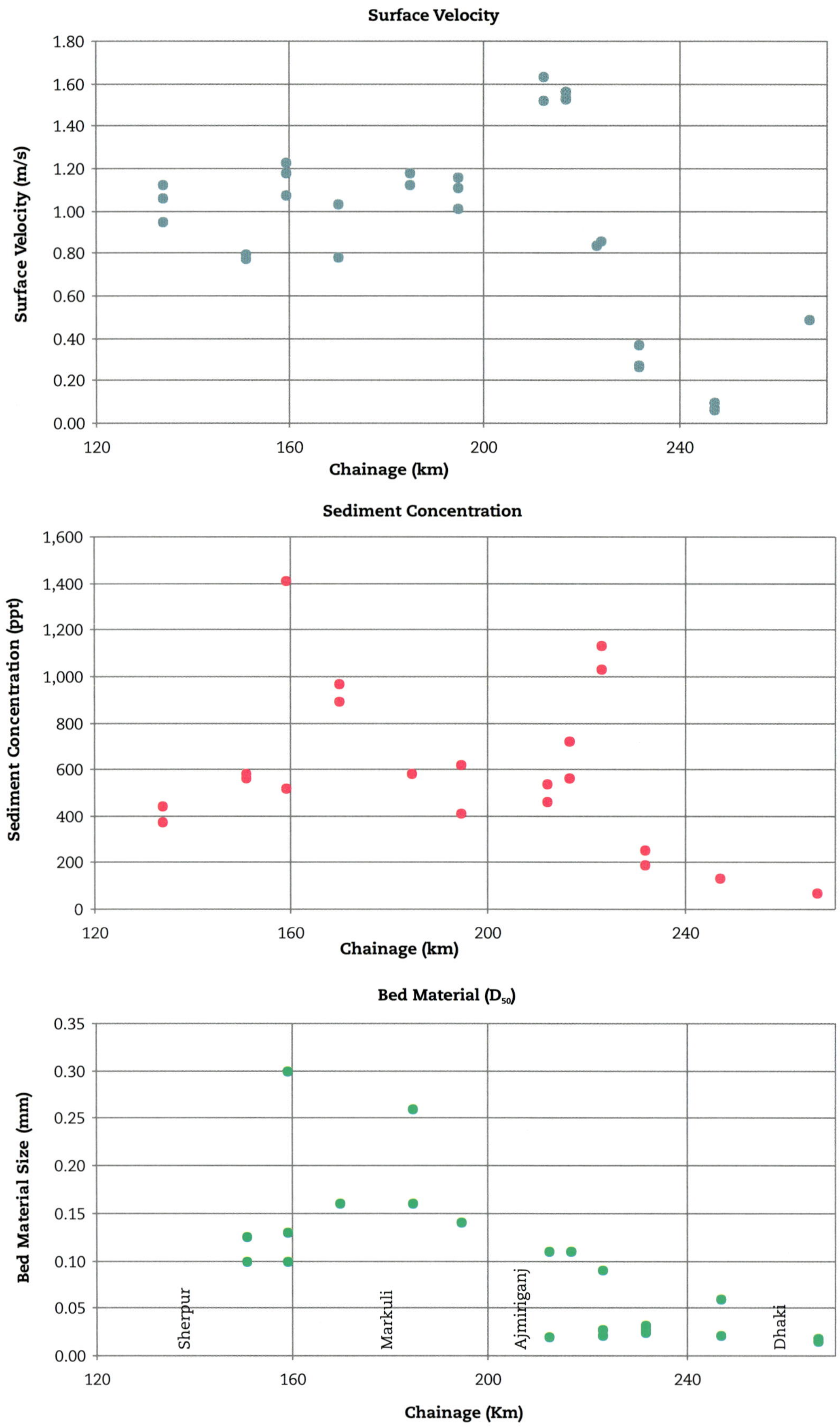

At the downstream of Ajmiriganj, due to high overbank flow, reduction of flow velocity within the river was very significant, which caused to reduce the sediment concentration. The minimum was found to be below 100 mg/l, where flow velocity was only 0.25 m/s.

The average size of D_{50} up to Ajminirganj was found to be 0.15 mm with minimum 0.1 mm to maximum 0.3 mm. At the downstream of Ajmiriganj, the size of bed material has reduced to 0.02 mm (Figure 6.12).

6.5 River Width

The distance between the riverbank lines perpendicular to the flow direction has been measured at 10 km interval for calculating the river width at bankfull stage. From Amalshid to Sherpur, the Kushiyara River is seen to vary its section width randomly from 100 to 200 m. The width is found to increase up to 250 m at Sherpur downstream of the confluence of the Manu River. These results are very much in line with the findings of FAP in the 1990s. Further downstream, the width of the river decreases and at the newly developing course, downstream of Katkhal, it goes below 100 m (Figure 6.13).

Reach-averaged width is maximum about 210 m in the middle reach from Sherpur to Markuli. It is minimum at about 140 m in the upstream and 170 m in the downstream reach which ends at Katkhal. The high width in the middle reach is the reflection of the combined flow of all its major tributaries. The decrease of reach-averaged width suggests the entrance into the Sylhet Basin.

6.6 Long Profile

The main function of a river is to transport water and sediment delivered from its catchment to the sea or lake. The river uses its potential energy acquired from its position to carry out its functions. Thus, the slope of the riverbed or riverbank plays an important role in fluvial processes. The Kushiyara River adopted this course about five to six decades ago. When a river enters into the Sylhet Basin it has to encounter high topographical gradient at the beginning followed by a flat terrain with almost no or negative gradient when it enters at the bottom of the Basin. The characteristics of the river with such changing conditions would be reflected from its long-profile analysis. The long profile of the Kushiyara River based on a BIWTA hydrographic survey, a BWDB cross-section survey and water level data is described in the following sections.

Hydrographic survey data of 2010 from the BIWTA have been used for presenting the long profile of the Kushiyara. Data of water level and bank level used by FAP 6 have been used to present it (Figure 6.14). The gradient of bank level is higher at the upstream and gradually becomes flatter at the downstream. The river slope starts to decrease as it enters into the Sylhet Basin. The rising of bed level and lowering of the bank from flood level coincide almost at the same location upstream of Ajmiriganj which is followed by a deeper reach at the downstream. Similar processes of rising of riverbed had been observed by CEGIS (2011) for the Surma River. The dry season gradient of water level profile at the shallow reach downstream of Ajmiriganj is very high. The bank levels of the Kushiyara River presented here are from one and a half decade old data. A new process of river avulsion had already been started since the mid-1990s. The bed profile presented in Figure 6.14 at the downstream of Khatkhal is from the old course. The data presented are not up to date or from the same period. This is one of the limitations to illustrating the river processes when it entered into the Sylhet Basin several decades ago.

Figure 6.13

Downstream Variation in the Width of the Kushiyara River

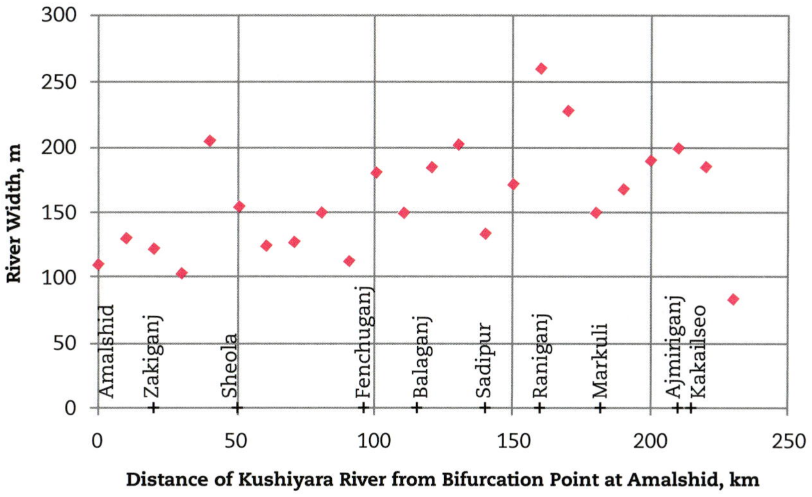

Source: CEGIS, 2011.

Figure 6.14
Long Profile of the Kushiyara River

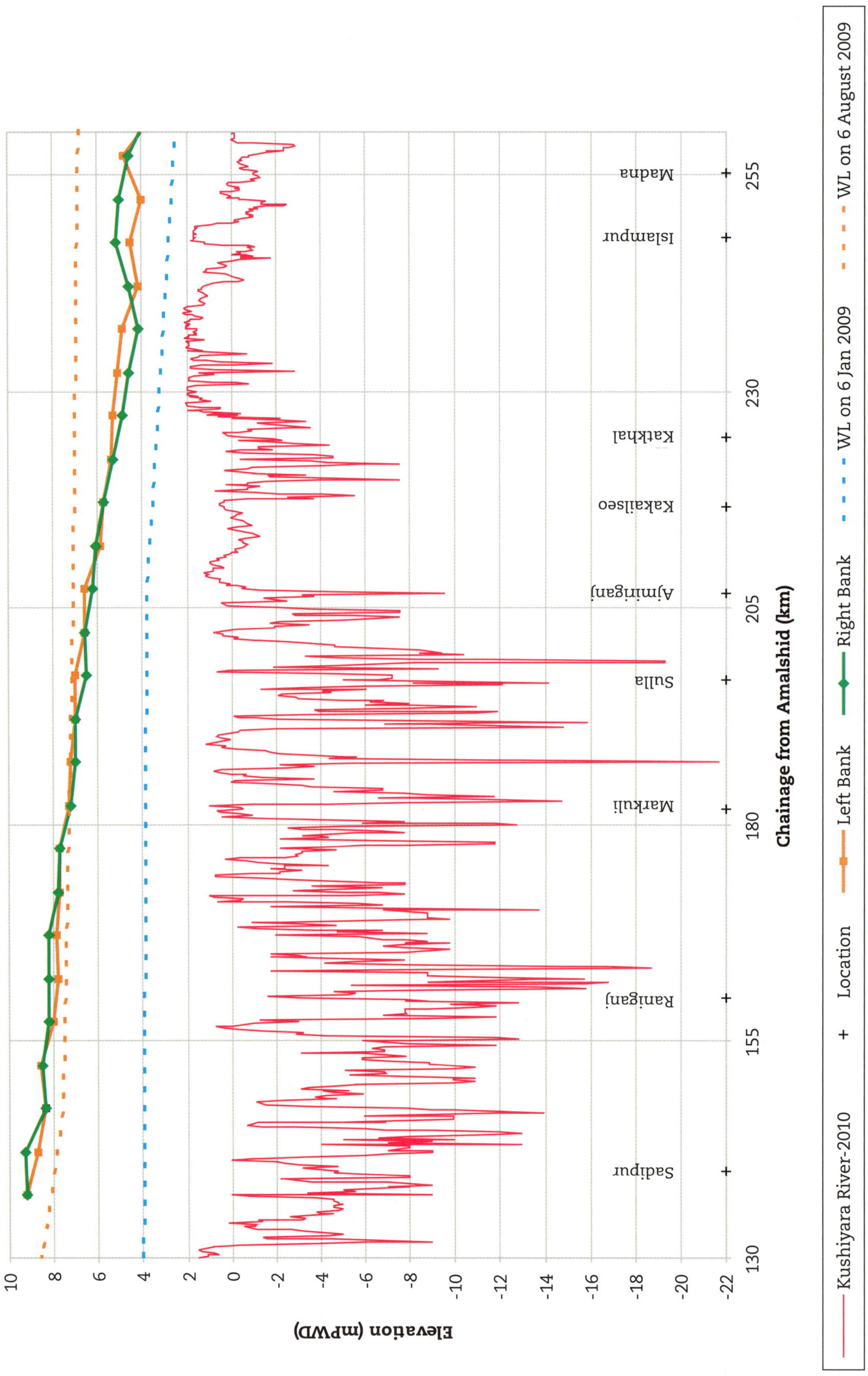

Source: CEGIS, 2011.

7

Development of Conceptual Model for the Rivers in Sylhet Basin

7.1 Model Development

CEGIS (2011) has developed a conceptual model to demonstrate the river evolution processes in the depressed Sylhet Basin, after they have shifted to their new courses. Availability of data for model verification is sparse. Under the contract with the IUCN, CEGIS measured flow velocity, sediment concentration and bed material samples from the downstream reaches of the Kushiyara River and these data were used to support the model. The model will be useful, however, for identifying the causes of deterioration of navigability in the Kushiyara River. It will help to assess future developments and to plan interventions for improving navigability.

It is assumed that the river reaches at the upstream of the Sylhet Basin are in regime condition. In most cases with natural rivers, the annual average flood is close but higher to the bankfull level (Chang, 1979) and flood profile is assumed to be parallel to the bank line. The gradient of the topography is flatter than that of the side slope of the Sylhet Basin, which varies 15 to 25 cm/km. However, the gradient of the bottom of the Sylhet Basin is very flat.

Due to the rapid subsidence and huge sediment supply from upstream, the rivers in the Sylhet Basin frequently avulsed from their existing courses. The model presented in Figure 7.1 shows the channel evolution after time t_1 from its avulsion, although the avulsion is not a suddenly occurring event; it also shows the final form of channels at time t_α, after completion of the evolution processes. Flood and low flow profiles after time t_1 of the river avulsion into the Basin bank are shown in Figure 7.2. As the traverse distance of the channel within the Basin increases, the gradient of the riverbank flattens and the difference in elevation between bank and flood level increases at a certain stage i.e., at the bottom of the Basin, the bank and flood profile become parallel with a considerable differences in elevation.

Channel dimensions are considered as the function of the dominant discharge and often bankfull discharge is considered as the dominant discharge (Chang, 1979; Bridge, 2003). The bankfull discharge of the channel in concern varies in the downstream direction (Figure 7.1A). At the upstream, it is high and close to annual average flood discharge. This implies that in most days in a year, the river flow is confined within the bank. On the other hand, the bankfull discharge at the downstream is much less and the overbank flow occurs for several months during the monsoon.

Decrease in the bankfull discharge at the downstream, however, indicates a decrease in channel dimensions i.e., the width and depth (Figure 7.1B). This might be the reason why the width of the river decreases while it enters into the Sylhet Basin as observed in the satellite images. Figure 7.1B shows the channel dimensions without any influence of sediment.

This simplified diagram as presented in Figure 7.1B, does not show the influence of sedimentation within the channel during monsoon when the discharge within channel and flow velocity start to decrease at the downstream. FAP 6 mentioned that only 25 per cent of monsoon flow is carried by the channel within the Basin. This process facilitates the sedimentation within the riverbed. Thus a considerable amount of sedimentation occurs within the riverbed, a part of which is expected to be washed away during flood recession when the flow is confined within the riverbank and have attained considerable flow velocity to erode a part of the sediment deposits during monsoon. Shallow depth and high velocity generally exert high shear stress also on the riverbank and result in a wider section than expected from bankfull discharge of the reach concerned. The processes of sedimentation on the long profile and channel dimensions at different reaches are shown in Figure 7.1C. The shallow depth caused to increase the high gradient during the dry season and thus increase the dry season water level at the upstream.

After several years/decades (at time t_α) as the river will be able to raise its levee and reach regime condition, the flood level will be close to the bank level (Figure 7.1D), i.e., bankfull discharge will be the same along the whole river stretch. The channel dimensions will be closed the same at the upstream and downstream and no sedimentation would be expected during monsoon.

Figure 7.1

Conceptual Model for Describing the Channel Evolution Processes in a Subsiding Basin

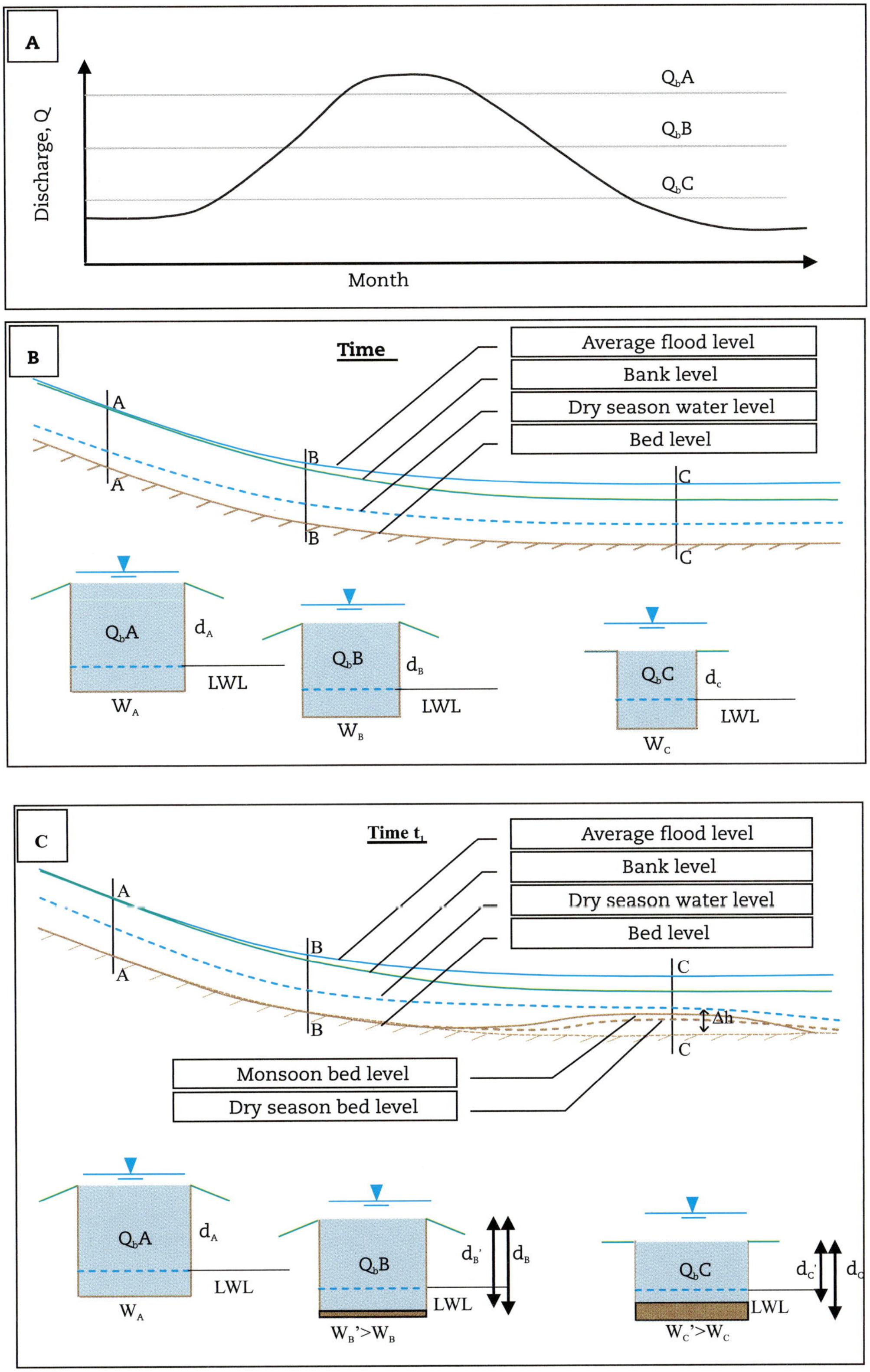

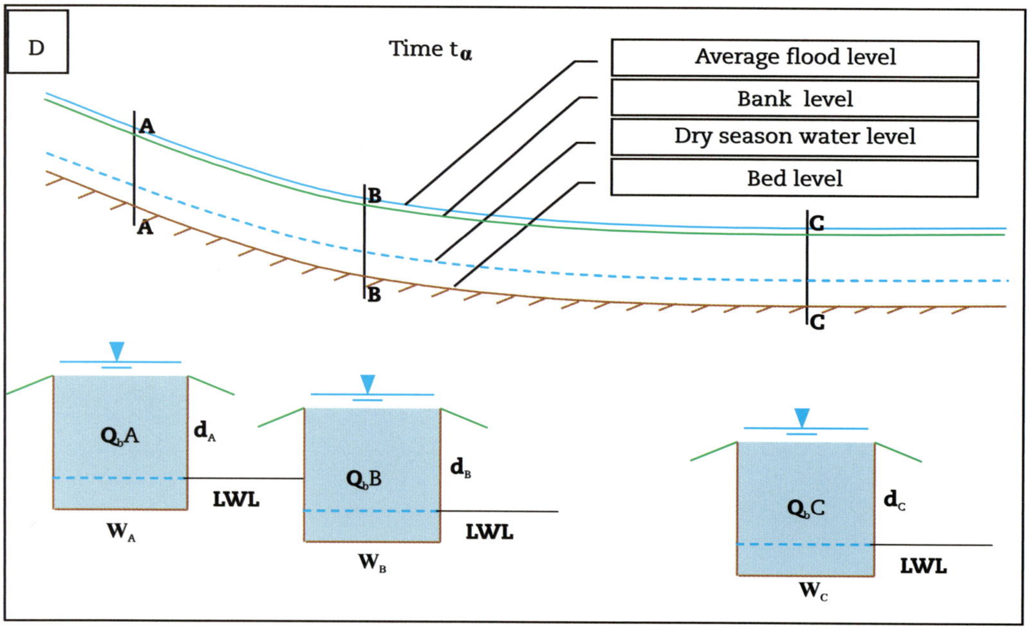

Note: (A) a simplified discharge hydrograph showing bankfull discharges of different reaches of the river at time t_1, (B) long profiles of river bank, riverbed, flood level and dry season water level at time t_1 without having any influence of sediment, (C) long profiles with the influence of sediment and (D) long-profiles at time t_α, when the river would be in regime condition.

Value of Δ h depends on sediment input

Figure 7.2

Simplified Diagram Showing the Relations between the Different Parameters such as Gradient, Bank Level, Flood Level, Flow Velocity, Sediment Concentration and Bed Material Size during Monsoon and Dry Season at Time t1.

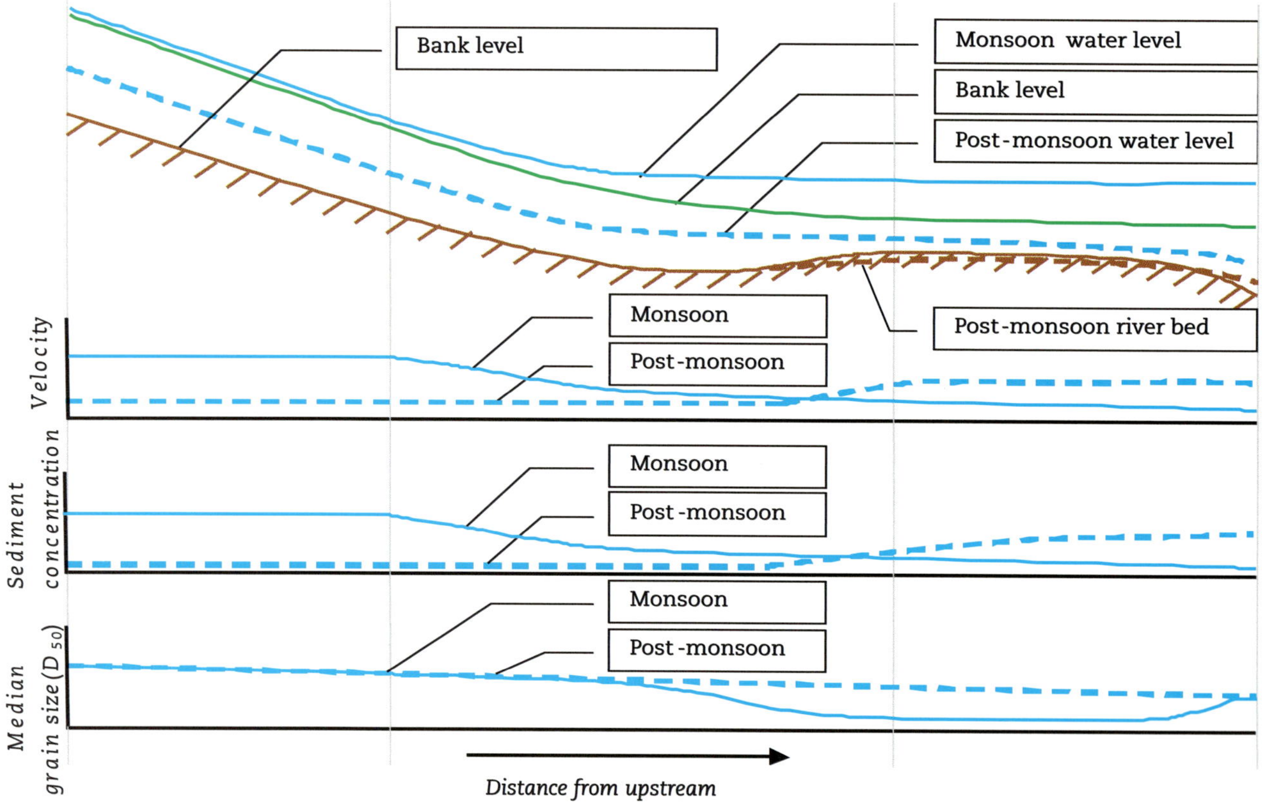

A simplified diagram is however, presented in Figure 7.2 for showing the spatial variation of river gradient, flood profile, bank profile, riverbed profile, flow velocity, sediment concentration, bed material sizes both in monsoon and dry season of a river, which is approaching towards regime conditions after its avulsion into the Sylhet Basin.

The long profile of the Kushiyara River (i.e., the modeled river) shows the flood, bank and bed profiles during monsoon. During monsoon, average flow velocity in the channel will remain the same within the upstream river reaches, which is in regime condition. As the overbank flow increases at the downstream, the flow velocity in the river reduces. The reduction of the flow velocity facilitates sedimentation within the river and thus reduces the sediment concentration substantially at the downstream. This explains the presence of the lower riverbed level at the downstream of depositing reaches, although the flow velocity remains very low at that reach also. Sediment concentration during monsoon at that location is too low to raise the riverbed through deposition.

At the end of monsoon, discharge reduces and water level remains at a stage lower than the bank level. The depositing reach will cause to produce back water effect at the upstream. The river is shallow at this reach and thus the gradient is much higher than at the upstream (Figure 7.2). Flow velocity at the upstream is much less than in monsoon, but it starts to increase at the depositing reach. This high velocity helps to erode a part of the depositing sediment during the preceding monsoon and thus increase the sediment concentration in the downstream direction.

Bed materials in the Surma and Kushiyara rivers are generally fine sand, but these materials are only 25 per cent of the total sediment transport in the river. The size of the transported sediment was found to be finer during the aggradation phase and coarser during the degradation phase (Miller and Benda, 2000; Bartley and Rutherfurd, 2005). Thus, the bed material during the monsoon in the depositing reaches would be finer but it would be coarser again during the end of monsoon when a part of the deposition is washed away.

The proposed model shows relations between the different parameters such as gradient, bank level, flood level and flow velocity, sedimentation process in the riverbed and floodplain and their spatial variation along the river which is in the way to reaching regime condition. During the evolution phase of the rivers in the Sylhet Basin the rivers adjust their morphology continuously. The process that triggers the progression of the whole process towards the downstream is the adjustment of the bank level. This process will cause to push the sediment deposited reaches to the downstream. The rivers will reach regime condition after time t_α, following which the bank level will be parallel to the annual average flood level (Figure 7.1D) and no bed aggradation/degradation will occur during monsoon or dry season.

It is unlikely that the rivers in the Sylhet Basin may reach regime conditions, as the subsiding Basin needs to have a high difference in elevation between the levee and flood Basin, which may cause avulsion of the rivers. Moreover, a major part of the river sediment deposits on the floodplain along rivers where the bank level starts to become lower than the annual average flood level. This may also trigger avulsion of the rivers towards the plain which is not getting sediment for a long time. The adjustment process of the rivers is not followed at the downstream only. The downstream adjustment also triggers flood and bank level adjustment at the upstream as well.

As the adjustment of river channels to any disturbance takes several years/decades, the rivers have to act with several disturbances simultaneously. The Kushiyara River has been adjusting to its avulsion to the present course for the last several decades, at the same time cut-offs in the 1980s and 1990s put the river into a simultaneous process of major adjustments. In the 1990s, a process of avulsion had already been started and the river also acted to adjust with the changes. Thus under natural conditions, the process would not be as straightforward as shown in the model (Figure 7.1) or in the simplified diagram (Figure 7.2). If the different disturbances in the river system are recognised properly the model would be helpful in explaining the different observed changes in rivers.

7.2 Model Verification

This model addresses the evolution of the river system in the Sylhet Basin. In this context, the different morphological processes observed in the Surma, the Kushiyara and other rivers in this Basin could be explained and future development of these rivers could be predicted if the model could be validated using a good number of data on flow velocity, sediment concentration, bed material size, recent monsoon and dry season bathymetries and higher temporal and spatial resolutions of satellite images, and recent bank level data on the rivers. Due to the limited scope of the study, it was not possible to collect primary data for verifying the model. At the most, the model can provide an indicative result only. However, available data on bed material samples of the Kushiyara River collected by FAP 6 could be used to support the model. CEGIS also carried out a data collection campaign in the Kushiyara River from 20 to 24 September 2011 in connection with a project of the IUCN. These data can be used to verify the model. A good amount of data will allow to improve the model and to make it usable for sustainable and effective interventions in the river system in the Sylhet Basin.

Several bed material samples along the Kushiyara River were collected both in monsoon and dry season by the FAP 6 study. Representative sizes (D_{50}) of the bed materials along the river course are presented in Figure 7.3. The upper boundary of the bed material size has a tendency to be finer at the downstream. However, from Markuli to the upstream of Madna, the size of the bed material shows very scattered results. FAP 6 mentioned that they had found coarser bed material during the dry season at these reaches. The proposed diagram to support the model also shows a large variation in the bed material in the sediment deposited reach. The FAP 6 data, however, support the model and also confirm that the deposition occurs during monsoon, and that a part of that sediment is washed away during the recession of flood.

The locations of the data sampling campaign conducted by CEGIS, 2011 in the Kushiyara River are shown in Figure 6.11. The campaign followed the newly developed course of the Kushiyara River, which meets with the Surma River at Dhaki. The average water levels at Markuli and Ajmiriganj during the data campaign were 7.5 and 7.2 mPWD respectively indicating that the river at these locations was flowing below bankfull level. Overbank flow was found downstream of chainage 180 km during the sampling campaign. The results

Figure 7.3

Bed Material Sizes (D_{50}) along the Kushiyara River

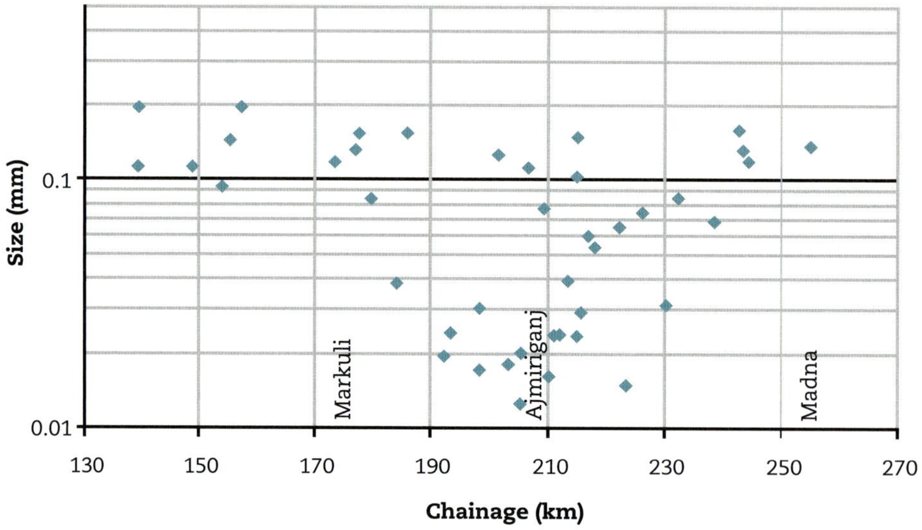

Source: SNC *et al.*, 1997, figure 33.

as presented in Figure 6.12 show that surface velocity upstream of Ajmiriganj was about 0.80 m/s. However, the flow velocity increased to 1.20 m/s in a few kilometers long stretch at the transition of over bank flow. It gradually started to decrease from where the river was flowing above bank level. Minimum flow velocity in the river was found close to zero at the immediate upstream of Dhaki. Surface velocity increased to 0.40 m/s in the Surma River. The sediment concentration and bed material (D_{50}) size were also found to decrease from the same location as the surface flow velocity. However, sediment concentration shows a few scatters in the downstream. Although not fully, data presented in Figure 6.12, has good agreement with that indicated in Figure 7.1. The results of CEGIS' data sampling campaign thus support the model presented in Figure 7.1.

8

Causes of Deterioration

8.1 Causes of Deterioration of Navigability

The navigability in the Kushiyara River was not perennial for large vessels of more than two meter draught; the duration of navigability however, has changed over time. During the 1970s, such duration was for six to seven months of the year, which had reduced in the 1990s. Analysis of water level and satellite images suggested that channel changes at downstream reaches of Ajmiriganj mainly caused the deterioration of navigability. This deterioration was however associated with the increase of pre-monsoon flood in the Kushiyara Basin. In a fluvial system several processes may act simultaneously, the effects of which may be of different magnitudes. The probable causes of deterioration of navigability are discussed in the following sections.

8.2 Channel Avulsion and Effects on Navigation

Several changes occurred in the Kushiyara course during the last three decades, such as development of cut-offs at the downstream of Ajmiriganj and upstream of Khatkhal, and avulsion of the Kushiyara to link with the Surma from Katkhal to the Dhaki. Every event has its impacts on the hydro-morphological processes of the river.

During the process of cut-off, there exists two parallel channels; the old channel is silting up along with subsequent enlargement of another newly developed channel. Generally, the geometry at the bifurcation governs the distribution of sediment among the downstream channels. High deviation angle from the upstream channel facilitates the entry of more sediment into the old channel than the newly developed channel thereby creating a low deviation angle. Times-series satellite images of 1984, 1990 and 1997 show the cut-off and initiation of avulsion processes of the Kushiyara River at the downstream of Ajmiriganj (Figure 8.1). A very high deviation angle (>300^0) of the right anabranch has caused sedimentation in the right channel and subsequent enlargement of the left channel.

The process of development of a channel needs more energy than a regime channel to transport the same flow and sediment as a part of the flow energy is spent on eroding the materials from its boundary layer. Moreover, in regime condition, the anabranching reach of a river requires a higher gradient than the single channel reach for transporting the same discharge and sediment (Leopold and Wolman, 1957). Thus the process of cut-off started in the early 1980s, downstream of Ajmiriganj and caused to increase the slope of a 7 km long reach, which affected the water level at the upstream. The effect was very much pronounced during dry season with diminishing effects during pre-monsoon flood. No effects could be felt during monsoon as the flow over the floodplain was much higher than the flow within the channel (Figure 7.1). Since the early 1980s dry season water level started to rise and continued for the next one decade. Thereafter dry season water level showed a stable pattern. From the early 1980s to early 1990s, the rise in dry season water level was about 1.7 m. A series of changes such as two cut-offs and one avulsion of the river channel through the Khatkhal-Dhaki channel (Figure 5.5) were mainly responsible for raising the dry season water level at Ajmiriganj. With the rising water level, tidal variation at Ajmiriganj was reduced sharply from 15 cm to 3 cm (Figure 6.9). The effects of the increase of dry season water level at Ajmiriganj also caused an increase of water level at Markuli and Fenchuganj (Figure 7.10) but it did not have any noticeable influence on the downstream water level such as at Madna.

Dry season water level profiles along the Kushsiyara River in the 1980s and 1990s (Figure 8.2) indicate a very high slope between Ajmiriganj and Madna, which represents constraints. The constraints were due to the availability of less depth during the process of cut-offs or avulsion.

Increase of Sediment

The Kushiyara River is heavily loaded with sediment, especially after joining with the tributaries such as the Manu, the Dhalai and the Khowai coming from the Tripura Hills. Time series sediment analysis has not been done to assess the changes in sediment regime. Deforestation and intensive agriculture practices have increased in this region in the last decades (Verghese, 1990). It is likely that sediment laden flow may cause frequent cut-offs or avulsion of the river courses. Moreover, increase of sediment also causes to decrease the depth

Figure 8.1

Cut-off and Initiation of Avultion Process Downstream of Ajmiriganj (Analysed by CEGIS, 2011a)

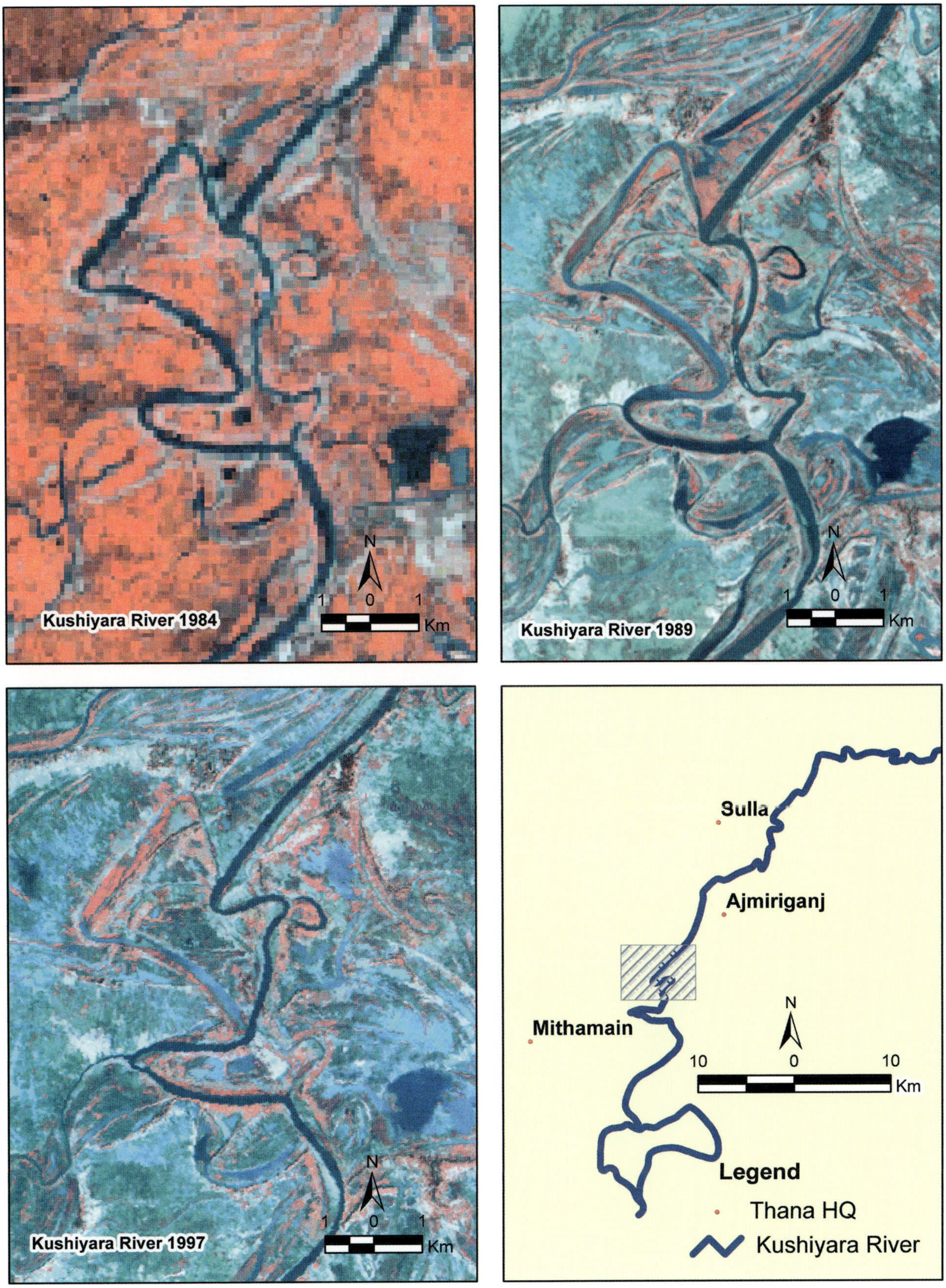

Figure 8.2

Dry Season Water Level Profile of the Kushiyara River in 1982 and 1993 showing the Changes in Gradient Downstream of Ajmiriganj (Analysed by CEGIS, 2011).

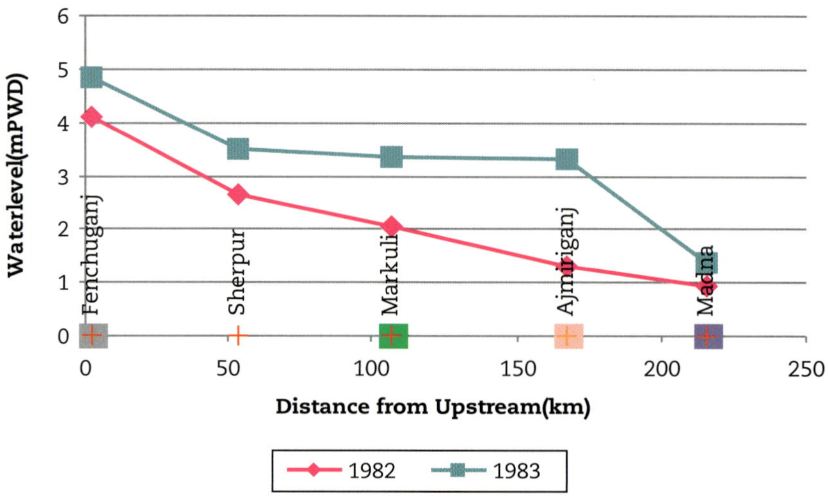

of the river channel as indicated in the model presented in Figure (7.1).

Human Interventions

The closure of the Mora Surma in the early 1980s increased the pre-monsoon and post-monsoon flow and may have accelerated the deterioration of the navigability of the Kushiyara River. There were several breaching of levees of the Kushiyara River during the last two decades at the downstream of Sherpur. The BWDB has closed those breaches but several repeated closings are required at some of the locations. These closures reduce the risk of avulsion or channel cut-offs. On the other hand, keeping the flow within the existing channel makes the system more dynamic. It is very difficult to assess the overall effect of these closures on the navigability of the river.

8.3 Deterioration of Traffic

The partition between India and Pakistan in 1947 also portioned the rivers between these countries. The river service to Assam using this route was stopped in 1965 when the Indian transit traffic was 115,000 tonne. Although it was reopened in 1973, the traffic has never recovered as the growth of railway occurred and later roads and centres of economic activities moved from the waterways (Verghese, 1990). Furthermore, the Kalni-Kushiyara river system is not navigable throughout the year. Recent sedimentation on the riverbed downstream of Ajmiriganj causes reduction of local traffic.

9

Future Development of Kushiyara Route

9.1 Assessing the Future Development

The future development of navigability and both passenger and cargo traffic have been assessed under different scenarios such as with autonomous development (without any human interventions and climate change), with human interventions such as the Tipaimukh Dam Project in India and the Kalni-Kushiyara River Management Project in Bangladesh, and with climate change.

9.2 Autonomous Development

For assessing the autonomous development of the navigability and navigation traffic of the Kushiyara River the prevailing physical condition and traffic conditions are projected. It is assumed that the there is no trend of change in dry season or monsoon flow in the river. Sediment load is assumed to be the same as it is now.

The cut-off or avulsion of the river will occur at the same frequency as it was during the last three decades. It may take the Dhaki Nala one to two decades to complete the avulsion process. It is expected that the dry season water level will be lowered at Ajmiriganj and Markuli in the Kushiyara River after completion of the avulsion process. The LAD will be increased at the downstream of Ajmiriganj significantly, but it may cause a decrease in LAD at the upstream.

Transit traffic will be reduced. After improving navigability in the coming decade transit cargos may not increase as the generated traffic may find alternative ways to move. However, in Bangladesh, especially in the Sylhet Basin, there is no alternative option for the generated traffic. Instead of decreasing, the traffic may increase in the future at the cost of the development of the region as the movement of both passenger and cargos have to face huge constraints as it is doing at present.

9.3 Impacts of Human Interventions

Human interventions may alter the flow and sediment regimes and thus the navigability and flood regimes of the river. Intensive agriculture or deforestation may increase the sediment input into the system which is a threat to navigation and would cause frequent breaching of levees, shifting of the river courses and spread of sediment over agricultural lands. Although sediments have several short-term negative effects, it plays a very positive role ultimately in compensating the subsidence in the Sylhet Basin. The threat of climate change may also cause to increase the positive demand of the sediment from upstream. Effective sediment management may mitigate the short-term negative effects of sediments. The diversion of water for irrigation will, however, deteriorate the navigability of the river unless the lean season flow is adequately augmented. In the following paragraphs, the impact of two large projects in India and Bangladesh are presented.

Tipaimukh Dam project

This is a multi-purpose water resources project that has been planned by the Government of India at Tipaimukh on the Barak river at its confluence with Tuvai river 200 km upstream from the border between Bangladesh and India. This project has now become a widely discussed undertaking both in India and Bangladesh. The project proposes a hydropower plant of 1500 MW capacity along with an irrigation potential of 100,000 ha. It will be located at the tri-junction of the states of Manipur, Assam and Mizoram.

Information about this project is very limited as the project report and data are "classified" and not available to the general public. The information presented here is taken from the FAP 6 Report (SNC *et al.*, 1993).

A very preliminary assessment of the potential impact of the Tipaimukh dam was previously provided by FAP 6. According to them, the dam could produce both positive and negative impacts. In the positive sense, it could reduce flooding and sediment flow in the monsoon season and in the negative sense, it could increase post-monsoon flow. Moreover, there is a large drainage area between Tipaimukh and Amalshid which receives the world's largest rainfall. So there is a strong probability that pre-monsoon flood affecting the project area are generated within this catchment.

If the dam becomes operational only for power generation without diverting the water for irrigation, it is likely that the dry season flow in the Kushsiyara River will be increased, which will help to improve the navigability of the river. However depending on the increase of dry season flow, it may have negative impacts on *Boro* crops in the Sylhet Basin. A well-balanced view needs to be taken considering the different factors impacted by dam operation.

Kalni-Kushiyara River Management Project

The Kalni-Kushiyara River Management Project (KKMRP) proposes a number of engineering interventions for integrated water management in the Sylhet Basin (the project is not fully implemented yet). In 1994, the Canadian International Development Agency (CIDA), along with the Flood Plan Coordination Organization (FPCO) and the Bangladesh Water Development Board (BWDB) decided to proceed with both a pilot dredging project and a feasibility study for KKMRP. The objectives of this project are:

- Improvement of the river's long term stability.
- Reduction of crop damage due to pre-monsoon flood.
- Improvement of living conditions along the floodplain by reducing erosion damage.
- Improvement of navigation during dry season.

The proposed intervention includes:

- Excavation of a portion of the river between Ajmiriganj and Madna.
- Bank protection works upstream of Ajmiriganj.
- Construction of low levees on the floodplain at low local riverbanks to help confine pre-monsoon spills.
- Construction of loop cuts near Khatkhal and Issapur to provide a more stable alignment, as well as increase the river's self-scouring capacity and help reduce water level.

Navigation will be significantly improved. According to FAP 6 improvement of the channel between Madna and Ajmiriganj will facilitate year round navigation for large mechanised vessels (BIWTA Class-II). According to the SNC *et al.*, 1993, improvement of the navigability of the river will result in an increase in both passenger and cargo traffic.

Impact of KKMRP

- Navigation will be significantly improved. According to FAP 6 improvement of the channel between Madna to Ajmiriganj will facilitate year round navigation for large mechanised vessels (BIWTA Class-II).
- The main commodities of freight traffic in this route are fertiliser, rice, building material, POL, food items, consumer goods, etc. Because of the successful implementation of the KKMRP, fertiliser demand will increase about 8 per cent and fertiliser rehandling through transit will increase 28 per cent.
- Fertiliser through trans-shipment will increase from 0 to 160000 tonne because of the presence of major fertiliser wholesalers within the projected area.
- The number of passengers will increase because of time and cost saving opportunities in dry season.

It is understood that within a short time, the BWDB is going to implement the project and start the physical interventions. By this time, the main course of the Kalni-Kushiyara River has been avulsed through the Dhaki Nala. The BWDB is conducting dredging to follow the abandoned course of the river. The river, however, will always have the tendency to avulse again from its old course. The avulsion process always causes decline of navigability and also increases pre-monsoon flood. Thus, dredging and other interventions may bring about a short-term benefit only.

9.4 Impact of Climate Change

Climate change is expected to be associated with sea level rise, changing precipitations and thus the changing of flow and sediment regimes of the rivers. These three aspects will have pronounced effects on the regimes of the Kushiyara River. The sea level rise and changes in the flow in sediment regimes will be a gradual process. With the changes of these parameters the river will try to adjust its morphology with the changed situation. The assessments of the effects of climate change are presented qualitatively in the following paragraphs assuming the active adjustment process of the river.

It is assumed that sea level rise would be 100 cm (IPCC, 2007 and Mote *et al.*, 2008) and rainfall will be increased by 20 per cent and cause 20 per cent increase of flood flow. It is likely that the sediment will be increased due to increased precipitations (Walling and Webb, 1996; Hovius, 1998; Zhu *et al.*, 2008). The water levels of the Kushiyara River both dry and monsoon season are mainly influenced by water levels at Bhairab Bazaar, which are also heavily controlled by the water levels in the confluence of the Padma and Meghna River at Chandpur. CEGIS (2010) shows that increase in water level at Chandpur or upstream due to sea level rise will not be limited through back water effects; morphological adjustment processes will also contribute to the increases in water level.

The increase in sediment and flood discharge as well as base discharge would contribute to increasing the dynamics of the river and thus frequently cause problems in navigation through shifting or avulsion of the river courses.

10

Ways to Sustainable Navigation in line with Integrated Water Resources Management (IWRM)

10.1 Advantages of Inland Navigation

Inland water transport (IWT) is a competitive alternative to road and rail transport. In particular, it offers an environment friendly alternative in terms of both energy consumption, and noise and gas emissions. Its energy consumption per km/tonne of transported goods is approximately 17 per cent of that of road transport and 50 per cent of rail transport. Its noise and gaseous emissions are modest. In addition, inland waterway transport ensures a high degree of safety, in particular when it comes to the transportation of dangerous goods. Finally, it contributes to the decongestion of the overloaded road network in densely populated regions. According to recent studies, the total external costs of inland navigation (in terms of accidents, congestion, noise emissions, air pollution and other environmental impacts) are seven times lower than that of road transport

An efficiently run IWT system has environmental and social benefits over other modes of freight transport. Utilisation of waterways for transport can, for each tonne-km carried, help minimise the loss of agricultural land, reduce congestion on roads, reduce road accident costs, reduce the average energy consumption of freight transport, and reduce the greenhouse gases (GHG) that are contributing to climate change. Sustainable overall transport policies in any particular country may therefore need, among other measures, to consider whether and how to alter the modal distribution of transport in an attempt to mitigate the social and environmental costs of other forms of transport, as well as to reduce aggregate carbon intensity.

10.2 Requirements Sustainability in IWT System

Sustainability in transport systems has financial and economic, operational, environmental, and social dimensions. The requirements for sustainability as defined by the World Bank in a recent study on the Chinese waterways (Paulamos *et al.*, 2009) are presented below:

- *Economic sustainability:* This depends on the availability and utilisation of economic resources to meet freight market needs in a way that provides positive economic value to society as a whole. Economic resources in the sector include adequate and reliable water resources (taking account of other water users), navigation channels that can handle efficient vessels and are free of impediments, effective engineering structures such as locks and ship-lifts, general and specialised ports, and an effective vessel fleet, etc.

- *Financial sustainability:* This requires that the IWT sector obtains sufficient and reliable income to enable it to pay for the construction, maintenance and operations necessary to meet the market needs. For transport service operators, financial sustainability depends mainly on commercial revenue from freight customers. For infrastructure providers, it depends on a mix of commercial revenue from infrastructure users and funding from governments.

- *Operational sustainability:* This means the management, technical and technological capability to construct IWT infrastructure, and operate and maintain an increasingly busy and sophisticated IWT transport system more safely, efficiently and reliably.

- *Environmental sustainability:* This requires that the IWT industry should meet ever-increasing public and political expectations of environmental performance, including energy efficiency and low carbon generation, as well as more stringent environmental regulations. It should conform to the emission norms.

- *Social sustainability:* This means trying to ensure that the IWT industry develops as a good neighbour with communities who live alongside waterways, and that IWT policies try to take account of livelihoods of barging families who live and work on the waterways.

In the Context of Integrated Water Resources Management (IWRM)

People, wildlife, planet life—all are related to rivers. Rivers are the life blood of the earth. So our rivers must be managed in an integrated manner precisely said through "Integrated Water Resource Management (IWRM)" to ensure adequate supply of quality water, to meet the peoples' socioeconomic needs: to increase water use efficiency, to promote preparedness nationally and internationally to avoid conflicts about water crisis. According to a widely used definition, the IWRM is a process which promotes the coordinated development and management of water, land and related resources in order to maximise the resultant economic and social welfare, paving the way towards sustainable development, in an equitable manner without compromising the sustainability of vital ecosystems (Global Water Partnership, 2000).

International Conference on Water and Environment (Dublin 1992) set up four guiding principles for IWRM. Principle one acknowledged the fresh water as a finite and vulnerable resource which is essential to sustain life, development and the environment. Principle two suggested water development and management should be based on a participatory approach, involving users, planners and policy-makers at all levels. Principle three recommended that women should play a central role in provision, management and safeguarding of water. Principle four suggested water has an economic value in all its competing uses and should be recognised as an economic and social good.

10.3 Goals of IWRM

The goal of IWRM principles is to achieve sustainable co-existence of human being and nature. It should be kept in mind that integration must be ensured in three dimensions—area, social hierarchy and time. All beneficiaries should work together to achieve the integration of these elements and dimensions. According to UN Summit in 2000, the goals of IWRM are: IWRM leads to reduce the loss producing from disrupted water supply and consequently, helps to increase income and reduce poverty by achieving equitable, sustainable and guaranteed access to water. It builds an environment for additional production that promotes employment and income by developing related sectors, internal and external investment and release of water. IWRM also contributes to better health of the people by creating sustainable drinking water supply and improving quality of water in rivers and other sources. It helps environmental management and recovery by recognising the principal role of water for ecosystems and ensuring release of water for environmental purposes. And finally by involving so many people, IWRM promotes water education and awareness.

The above paragraphs describe the general principles and goals of IWRM in context of any water resource management project plan. However, for a particular route or particular region there are several socioeconomic and environmental aspects which may conflict with or favour the processes of improving the navigability of natural rivers. These aspects should be addressed properly through the IWRM framework.

10.4 In Context of IWRM Navigation in Kalni-Kushiyara

The length of the Kushiyara and Kalni-Kushiyara River is about 250 km in Bangladesh. Therefore, any measures to maintain or improve the navigation in this route have adverse or positive effects on different sectors such as agriculture, fisheries, environment and communication. By ensuring navigation, we actually ensure water for river to make it clean and healthy.

Kalni-Kushiyara is an important habitat for a large variety of animals and plants. Fish, amphibians, birds, insects, and reptiles live in this river, or adjacent *haor* areas find their food in this river. It plays a vital role in connecting habitats both between upstream and downstream areas, and by connecting both sides of river banks. Fish life and other aquatic flora and fauna need natural water flows within river banks and connectivity of habitats within the wider surroundings (*haor*) for their survival. Natural water flows also promote biological purification processes that contribute to cleaner water in support of life. By ensuring navigation we also ensure the natural flow for the river.

During the last couple of decades it has been found that the dry season and pre-monsoon water levels in the Kushiyara River upstream of Ajmiriganj has increased. As pointed out in Chapter 8, this increase in dry season and pre-monsoon water level are due to the shifting and/or avulsion of the Kushiyara River, which thus create problems for navigation and damage *boro* crops. Most of the people living around the route are involved with crop production. Dredging in the Kushiyara River to expedite the avulsion process will improve navigability and reduce the frequency of pre-monsoon floods and ensures water all-round the year throughout the route. Moreover drainage improvements in post-monsoon period will also increase the land availability for timely plantation of *boro* crops. Farmers will be able to utilise the soil moisture for *rabi* crop cultivation. The submergible levees along the river to protect *boro* crops will confine more flow within the channel. The conceptual model shown in Figures 7.1 and 7.2 suggests that it would help to maintain the navigability of the river.

Communications of a large number of people living in the Sylhet Basin are fully dependent through navigation during the monsoon. Road communication was very poorly developed in the Basin area due to its special topographical characteristics. In the dry season most of the people do not have any formal means of communication other than mechanised vehicles (motorbikes, four-wheeled mechanised vehicles). However, these vehicles have limitations to carrying large amounts of bulk material. During the last couple of decades, a few interventions such as submergible embankments for protecting *boro* crops (the only major crops) from pre-monsoon floods may have also restricted the navigation connectivity between the flood Basin areas with the river. Local informal navigation had to compromise with the interest of agriculture. Ensuring navigation in Kalni Kushiyara all-round the year will improve the access to more remote areas during post-monsoon and will inevitably generate additional commercial activity. Thus, it increases both direct and indirect employment opportunities. It will also include additional employment for boat-crews.

The increased channel depth from dredging and alleviation of channel siltation will increase fish production within the channel as it will increase the wet surface making it favourable for fish during during dry season. The flooded area during the pre-monsoon will be reduced. However, pre-monsoon flooding is extremely important for fish breeding, so it may be hampered. Along with reduction of bank spills and breaches of river bank, the productivity of *haor* fish may also be reduced. Since the monsoon water-level will not be affected by dredging, the impact on aquatic flora and fauna will be insignificant.

The sectors have to meet the challenge of how to remain successful in a changing world. The solutions should reinforce and build upon the successes, while mitigating adverse side-effects and anticipating and accommodating future changes.

10.5 Conditions for Accepting IWT Sector as Preferable Mode of Transport

The IWT will become an 'acceptable mode' when the following conditions are met:

IWT–Cost	Substantially cheaper than road transport Comparable with rail
IWT–Time of Transportation	More than roadway but comparable with rail.
IWT–Reliability	Same or better than rail.
IWT–Safety of Cargo	Same or better than rail.

Once this is achieved, the shift in mode becomes voluntary, dictated by market forces and not by enforcement or by subsidy. The above conditions can be achieved if each component of the IWT, namely Fairway, Fleet, Navigational Aids and Terminals are properly planned, provided and maintained. IWT cost has two components: operating cost on account of fuel, crew wages, berthing and loading, repair and maintenance, and capital cost of the vessel.

Time of transportation has four components: waiting time for charter, loading time, sailing time and berthing/unloading time. Demand for IWT mode will determine the waiting time for charter.

Proper berth and loading /unloading facilities will reduce the loading time while unrestricted and well-defined fairways with day and night navigation facility will reduce sailing time.

Reliability of services depends on maintaining the sailing schedules without breakdown or hold-ups and ensuring efficient cargo receipt and delivery. Proper upkeep of vessels and maintenance, and management of the waterway are the components determining the reliability of services.

Safety of cargo involves safe storage handling and storage at origin and destination, safe handling and storage onboard the vessel, and safety from theft, pilferage and piracy.

The requirements leading to a condition of IWT acceptance can be summed up as follows:

- Unrestricted and well-defined fairway/channel with adequate depth, width and under keel clearance for round the year operation.
- Facility for sailing day and night (24 hrs navigation).
- Berthing facility at all stages of river with minimum vertical and horizontal transfer at reasonable cost and for different types of cargo (bulk, POL, containers etc.).
- Access/egress to road/rail for intermodal connectivity.
- Loading facility at required rate.
- Storage/bunkering and repair facility at terminals.
- Vessel assistance (river charts, river notice, navigation aids, tug assistance etc.).

10.6 Improvement of Navigation through Ashuganj-Karimganj Route

Based on the analysis presented in the report, the following recommendations are presented to maintain sustainable navigation in the Ashuganj-Karimganj route.

10.6.1 Improving the Navigability

To maintain perennial navigation for 1.8 m draught vessels the following are the recommendations:

- The constraints of navigation as identified downstream of Ajmiriganj should be removed, mainly through dredging. Navigability of the river would be restored gradually even if nothing is done, but it may take a couple of decades. Dredging in the newly developed channel may expedite the avulsion process and restore navigability.
- Recurrent maintenance dredging with a limited scale should be done upstream of Ajmiriganj to maintain perennial navigation in the river.
- All the physical interventions to improve and maintain navigability should be within the IWRM framework.
- Monitoring of the morphological processes and assessment of the LAD through hydrographic surveys should be carried out regularly.
- A study should be taken up to define the recurrent dredging procedure and for managing dredge spoil.
- Stabilisation and rectification of the river by appropriate river training works should also be taken up as a parallel action.

10.6.2 Improving the Navigation Aids and Safety

For easy navigation and to facilitate both passenger and cargo traffic the following actions are recommended:

- Marking of the channel with lighted buoys for day and night navigation.
- Regular river charts and river notices.
- Protocol clearances and customs formalities with minimum time loss.
- GPS/DGPS with electronic charts and up gradation of crew standards.

- Provision of terminals with adequate loading/unloading facilities, and
- Up gradation and augmentation of fleet.

10.6.3 Amendment of the Provisions of the Protocol

To increase traffic through the protocol route the following amendments of the Protocol Agreements between Bangladesh and India are suggested:

- The protocol routes 3, 4, 7 and 8 should be extended from Karimganj to Silchar in the Article 1.2
- Article 2.1 should incorporate a mandatory provision for both the countries to install night navigation facilities along the protocol routes (modalities or sharing of costs may be worked out).
- Article 11 should be replaced by the following: One country will provide customs services to the vessels in operation under the Protocol at or near points of entry and exit of the country and the vessels shall be allowed to load or unload at any place along the protocol route.
- Prohibition on vessels carrying transit cargo should be repealed from the Article 17.
- In order to provide a long-term assurance on return on investment to the private sector, the renewal of protocol may be made every 5 years instead of the existing 2 years period.

10.6.4 Private Sector Participation

The private sector has a major role in creation of IWT infrastructure. The IWT Policy of India, 2001 has many concessions for the private sector for investment in the sector which inter alia include:

- Vessel building subsidy.
- Government participation with private sector for joint ventures (JVs).
- Foreign direct investment (FDI).
- BOT projects with long concession periods.
- Viability gap funding
- Vessel leasing companies

The competent authorities, the BIWTA and the IWAI, may consider joint strategy for mobilisation of private sector investment for creation of IWT infrastructure and for IWT fleet augmentation.

10.7 Ways to Incorporate the Necessary Amendments to Maintain a Sustainable Navigation Route

Under Article 26 of the protocol of IWT and trade, there exists one standing committee with the representatives of both the governments for evaluation and review of the working of the protocol and for the purpose of improving IWT between the two countries. The suggested measures along with the proposed amendment of the Protocol may be put forward to both the governments (ministries of shipping in Bangladesh and India) for discussion at the meeting of the standing committee. After discussion its findings will be forwarded to the respective governments.

The findings of the standing committee may be further discussed in the upcoming meeting for renewal of the protocol. The bilateral renewal meeting at the level of secretaries to the governments decides everything regarding protocol. So the proposed amendment of the Protocol and suggested measures of development of inland navigation in the river Kushiyara must be forwarded to both the governments, so that both the countries may interact on it and take appropriate decisions.

10.8 Towards Sustainable Inland Navigation: Ashuganj-Karimganj Route

IWT is the most environmentally and economically sustainable mode of transport. This study focused on the sustainability of inland navigation along the protocol route Ashuganj to Karimganj in the north-eastern part of Bangladesh and India in line with IWRM. This was a joint research initiative conducted by a team comprising members representing Bangladesh and India. The joint research team worked together to find out the hindrances and constraints in the physical process of the river and in policy to make it a sustainable route. Most of the findings of this research should be considered as indicative. However, it provides an outline based on which future research can be done.

The route mainly covers the Kalni-Kushiyara River. Most part of the river is in the subsiding Sylhet Basin. This subsidence has a pronounced effect on the shifting or avulsion process of the river course and morphology. Historical maps indicate that the shifting of the courses of the Kushiyara in the last 240 years followed a particular direction towards the north, where the rate of subsidence was the maximum. Such an avulsion has also occurred at the downstream of Ajmiriganj even in the last two decades. This avulsion diverts the Kushiyara flow into the Surma River and reduces dry season water depth at the downstream of Ajmiriganj. This cut-off and avulsion has a great effect on navigation. It makes the dry season water level high at Ajmiriganj including at the upstream. This process has a huge impact in terms of deteriorating the navigability of the river. Moreover, this route suffers from the lack of maintenance causing it to degrade at a faster rate.

The Cachar-Narayanganj route had been operative from the colonial period, but it was discontinued for a couple of decades during the Pakistan regime. Although it was re-opened in 1973 after the liberation war of Bangladesh, the traffic has never recovered. The growth of railway, and later roads, moved the centres of economic activities from the waterways.

The future development of navigability of both passenger and cargo traffic has been assessed under different scenarios such as with autonomous development (without any human interventions and climate change), with human interventions such as the Tipaimukh Dam Project in India and the Kalni-Kushiyara River Management Project in Bangladesh, and with climate change. After assessing all the scenarios it can be concluded that under this prevailing protocol agreement, transit traffic will be reduced in the future but domestic traffic may be increased if the route can be maintained regularly.

It is assumed that due to climate change, sea level rise would be 100 cm and rainfall will be increased by 20 per cent and cause 20 per cent increase of flood flow and sediment. The water levels of the Kushiyara River both in dry and monsoon seasons are mainly influenced by water levels at Bhairab Bazaar. The increases in water level at Chandpur or the upstream due to sea level rise will not be limited through back water effects; morphological adjustment processes will also contribute to the increases in water level.

Ensuring navigation would also ensure a clean and healthy river environment. It will ensure the natural flow of the river. Communication and economic activities of the people living in Sylhet basin will also improve if navigation can be guaranteed during the dry season. It will help increase *Boro* production, and fish production within the channel will increase especially during the dry season.

Based on the analysis presented in the study some recommendations are made on improving the navigability, amending the provisions of the protocol, improving navigation aids and safety, and increasing private sector participation. All the recommendations are based on the concepts of sustainability and IWRM.

The constraints of navigation as identified downstream of Ajmiriganj should be removed, mainly through dredging. Recurrent maintenance dredging should be done at a limited scale at the upstream of Ajmiriganj to maintain perennial navigation in the river. At the same time, a study should be taken up to define the recurrent dredging procedure and for managing dredge spoil. Monitoring of the morphological processes and assessment of the LAD through hydrographic surveys should be carried out regularly. Stabilisation and rectification of the river by appropriate river training works should also be taken up as a parallel action. The protocol routes should be extended from Karimganj to Silchar. A mandatory provision should be made for both the countries to install night navigation facilities along the protocol routes. The private sector may take on a major role in establishing IWT infrastructure. For this purpose, joint ventures between the government and the private sector should increase. BOT projects should operate with long concession periods. Finally, both the government and the private sector should take necessary steps for addressing the gaps in their efforts to enhance regional cooperation.

References

Bartley, R. and I. Rutherfurd (2005). "Re-evaluation of the Wave Model as a Tool for Quantifying the Geomorphic Recovery Potential of Streams Disturbed by Sediment Slugs", *Geomorphology* 64: 221-42.

Bridge, J.S. (2003). *Rivers and Floodplains: Forms, Processes and Sedimentary Record*. Malden, USA: Blackwell Publishing. p.491.

Burnett, A.W. and S.A. Schumm (1983). "Alluvial-River Response to Geotectonic Deformation in Louisiana and Mississipi", *Journal Science*, 222: 49-50.

CEGIS (Center for Environmental and Geographic Information Services) (2011a). *Convergence of Inland Navigation and Integrated Water Resources Management Goals*. Draft final report.

————. (2011). "Development Area: Morphology", Vol. 2, *Master Plan of Haor Areas*. Prepared for Bangladesh Haor and Wetland Development Board

————. (2010). *Impact of Climate Change on Morphological Processes in Different River of Bangladesh*. Prepared for Asian Development Bank, Dhaka, Bangladesh.

Chang, H.H. (1979). "Geometry of Rivers in Regime", *Journal of the Hydraulics Division* 105(Hy6): 691-706.

DHV Consultants, Witteveen+Bos Consulting Engineers, BETS, Bangladesh (1989). *Inland Water Transport Masterplan (BIWTMAS)*. Final Report, Vol. 1. Prepared for Bangladesh Inland Water Transport Authority.

Global Water Partnership (2000). "Integrated Water Resources Management", *Technical Advisory Committee Background Paper* No 4. Stockholm: Global Water Partnership.

Griffiths P.J. (1979). *A History of the Joint Steamer Companies*. UK: Inchcape & Co. Limited

Goodbred Jr., S.L. and S.A. Kuehl (2000). "Enormous Ganges-Brahmaputra Sediment Discharge during Strengthened Early Holocene Monsoon", *Geology* 28: 1083-86.

Hovius, N. (1998). "Controls on Sediment Supply by Large Rivers", in K.W. Shanley and P.J. McCabe (eds.), *Relative Role of Estuasy, Climate, and Tectonism in Continental Rocks*. SEPM Special Publication 59. pp.3–16.

IPCC (2007). "Global Climate Projections", in *Climate Change 2007: The Physical Science Basis*. Contribution of Working Group I to the Fourth Assessment Report of the Intergovernmental Panel on Climate Change. Cambridge and New York: Cambridge University Press.

IUCN (International Union for Conservation of nature) (2011). "Convergence of Inland Navigation and Integrated Water Resources Management Goals", *Research Proposal*.

Leopold, L.B. and M.G. Wolman (1957). "River Channel Patterns: Braided, Meandering and Straight", *U.S. Geological Survey Professional Paper* 282 (B): 97-116.

Miller, D.J. and L.E. Benda (2000). "Effects of Punctuated Sediment Supply on Valley-floor Landforms and Sdiment Transport", *GSA Bulletin* 112: 1814-24.

Morgan, J.P. and W.G. McIntire (1959). "Quaternary Geology of the Bengal Basin, East Pakistan and India", *Geological Society of America Bulletin* 70: 319–42.

Mote, P., A. Petersen, S. Reeder, H. Shipman and L. Whitely Binder (2008). *Sea Level Rise in the Coastal Waters of Washington State*. Report prepared by the Climate Impacts Group. Seattle, Washington: University of Washington and Lacey, Washington: Washington Department of Ecology.

Netherlands Engineering Consultants (1967). *Inventoraization of the Waterways, Part-A, Classification Traffic and Fleet*, Vol.2. Prepared for East Pakistan Inland Water Transport Authority, Dhaka.

Ministry of Development North Eastern Region (2008). "General Strategies for the Region", *North Eastern Region Vision 2020*. Vol. 1.

Paualamos, Jiadashan, Sunjunyan Ningtao and Feiweijun (2009). *Sustainable development of Inland Waterway Transport Development in China*. Prepared for World Bank and the Ministry of Transport, People's Republic of China.

Schumm, S.A., J.F. Dumont and J.M. Holbrook (2000). *Active Tectonics and Alluvial Rivers*. UK: Cambridge University Press. p.276.

SNC, Lavalin International, Northwest Hydraulic Consultations, Engineering and Planning Consultations Ltd, Bangladesh Engineering and Technological Services (1998a). *Kalni-Kushiyara River Management Project Feasibility Study*. Final Report, Main Report, Vol. 1. Northeast Regional Water Management Project (FAP 6). Prepared for Water Resources Planning Organization (WARPO), Dhaka, Bangladesh.

————. (1998b). *Kalni-Kushiyara River Management Project Feasibility Study*, Annex-G, Final Report, Main Report, Vol. 1. Northeast Regional Water Management Project (FAP 6). Prepared for Water Resources Planning Organization (WARPO), Dhaka, Bangladesh.

————. (1998c). *Kalni-Kushiyara River Management Project Specialist Study*, Final Report, Main Report, Vol. 1. Northeast Regional Water Management Project (FAP 6). Prepared for Water Resources Planning Organization (WARPO), Dhaka, Bangladesh.

————. (1997). *Kalni-Kushiyara River Management Project Feasibility Study*, Annex-A, Draft Final Report, Main Report , Vol. 1. Northeast

Regional Water Management Project (FAP 6). Prepared for Water Resources Planning Organization (WARPO), Dhaka, Bangladesh.

———. (1993). *Kalni-Kushiyara River Management Project Feasibility Study*, Draft Final Report, Main Report, Vol. 1. Northeast Regional Water Management Project (FAP 6). Prepared for Water Resources Planning Organization (WARPO), Dhaka, Bangladesh.

Verghese, B.G. (1990). *Waters of Hope*. Vol-1. Dhaka: Bangladesh University Press Ltd. p.496.

Walling, D. E. and B.W. Webb (1996). "Erosion and Sediment Yield: A Global Overview", in D.E. Walling and B.W. Webb (eds.), *Erosion and Sediment Yield: Global and Regional Perspective*. Wallingford, UK: IAHS Publishing, IAHS Press. p.236.

Zhu, Y.M., X.X. Lu and Y. Zhou (2008). "Sediment Flux Sensitivity to Climate Change: A Case Study in the Long Changing Catchment of the Upper Yangtze River, China", *Global and Planetary Change* 60 (3–4): 429–42.

Annexes

ANNEX-1

Convergence of Inland Navigation and Integrated Water Resources Managenent Goals

CHECKLIST:

1. What was the condition of navigation depth?

80's		*90's*		*2011*		*Future*
Monsoon	*Dry*	*Monsoon*	*Dry*	*Monsoon*	*Dry*	

2. Size & number of vehicle (Cargo & Passenger):

80's		*90's*		*2011*		*Future*
Monsoon	*Dry*	*Monsoon*	*Dry*	*Monsoon*	*Dry*	

3. Origin and destination of vehicle (Cargo & Passenger):

80's	*90's*	*2011*	*Future*

4. Does any transit passenger/traffic use the present route? If any, then what is the amount?

5. What will be the effects of improvement by dredging in this route?

Goods		*Passenger*		*Traffic/Vessel*		*Depth of river*		
Monsoon	*Dry*	*Monsoon*	*Dry*	*Monsoon*	*Dry*			

6. What do you think about the implementation of the plan of over all improvement of navigation in this route?

ANNEX-2

A History of Navigation in the GBM River System

Before the advent of road and railways, the rivers were used extensively for transport of goods and passengers and great civilisations took their root on the river banks. India in its early history was a great sea faring nation and its trade extended as far as Greece and Macedonia in the west and Java in the east. The Greek traveller Magasthenese who came to India 2000 years ago described the Ganga and the Indus with their tributaries as navigable. Even as early as 14th century A.D navigation along rivers, canals and other water courses was a flourishing trade and a major means of communication. Rennel, in his book "Map of Hindoostan or the Mugul Empire in the Year 1792" says, "The Ganga and Burrampooter rivers together with their numerous branches and adjuncts intersect the country of Bengal in such a variety of directions, as to form the most complete and easy inland navigation that can be conceived."

Mechanically Propelled Vessels

The Ganga-Brahmaputra-Meghna (GBM) river system apart from being one of the largest river basins, also provide a vast network of navigational routes for inland vessels. Navigation in these routes by mechanically propelled vessels started in early 1800.

Almost two centuries ago, steam gun-boat *Diana,* set out from Calcutta on an epic voyage. Her destination lay well over a thousand miles distant. When the *Diana* finally dropped anchor, she lay in the shadow of the Himalayan foothills, barely 60 miles from India's north-east frontier with Tibet. The first voyage up one of the great rivers of eastern India had been successfully completed. *Diana* which weighed 89 tonnes, sailed with passengers from Kulpi Road to Calcutta, a distance of 50 miles on the Hoogly in 1823. Others followed in the *Diana's* wake, exploring not only the Brahmaputra but the Ganges, its tributaries and the vast network of waterways in East Bengal which form the combined delta of these mighty rivers.

Barak-Surma-Kushiyara System

The Surma-Meghna River System rises in the Manipur Hills of northeast India as the Barak River and flows west becoming the Surma River and then flows south as the Meghna River, a total of 946 km (669 km within Bangladesh) to the Bay of Bengal. The Meghna is formed inside Bangladesh above Bhairab Bazar by the combination of the Surma and Kushiyara rivers. After the Padma joins, it is referred to as the Lower Meghna. In Daudkandi, Comilla, Meghna is joined by the great river Gumti, created by the combination of many streams. This river reinforces Meghna a lot and increases the waterflow considerably The name for the largest distributary of the Ganges in Bangladesh is the Padma River. When the Padma joins with the Jamuna River, the largest distributary of the Brahmaputra, and they join with the Meghna in Chandpur District, after Chandpur, with the combined flow of the Padma and Jamuna, it moves South to join the Bay of Bengal.

Ashuganj and Karimganj

The research focuses on the sustainability of the international navigation route between Ashuganj and Karimganj: north-eastern part of Bangladesh and India. Presently, the Karimganj-Pandu is an important navigation route under the protocol between Bangladesh and India on Inland Water Transit and Trade. A stretch of this route in Bangladesh is considered primarily for Indian transit traffic and the Government of India pays an agreed amount of money to Bangladesh toward maintenance cost. The Surma Kushira rivers also provide connectivity to the hinterland in the intra Bangladesh traffic. Therefore, sustainability of this route is an important issue for inland navigation for both the countries.

Historic Routes

The Asunganj-Karimganj route is an integral part of this inland water transport network In 1900 A.D., three services operated in Cachar: Cachar Main Line, Cachar Despatch and Cachar Mail (Weekly). They operated from Calcutta to Fenjuganj during low water season and up to Karimganj during rainy season. The feeder routes included Fenjuganj-Karimganj and Fenjuganj–Chatak.

Upper reaches of the Ganges in the Bhagirathi had inadequate navigable depth, except for a few weeks in the peak of the annual flood season, so the pioneer navigators went downstream instead and just north of Saugor Island in the Hooghly estuary, they found a creek which led off eastwards into the maze of waterways of the Ganges-Brahmaputra delta known as the Sunderbans. The route through the Sunderbans is still the main navigation route to stations in Brahmaputra. Today it is part of the Indo-Bangladesh Protocol route.

Navigation in Early Days

Once clear of the Sunderbans and beyond the town of Khulna, the route was more straightforward. Even then, the Bakerganj district of East Bengal was largely settled and cultivated; the choice of waterways was not so great and although the Meghna estuary below Narayanganj—five miles from shore to shore—might seem to us an inland sea, it probably presented few problems to men whose only training had been in ocean navigation.

North-west of the Meghna and beyond Goalundo at the confluence of the Ganges and Brahmaputra, an altogether different set of problems faced the inland navigator. No longer was he confined to tortuous cross-connected creeks; here were vast rivers, the banks of which were rarely less than two miles apart. But where the creeks or the Delta had invariably carried more than sufficient navigable depth, the muddy waters of the Ganges and the Brahmaputra concealed only one rather mile upon mile of shoal area which there was perhaps only inches of water. Here, nothing was stable or well defined. Today's channel could be tomorrow's sand-bar. Current speeds could vary from a sluggish two-knots to the roaring twelve-knot spates of the annual flood season when a steamer might struggle for days to proceed less than a mile. There were few fixed landmarks. Not even the main banks of the river could be relied upon; they could move hundreds of yards—in a single season and in the annual floods, would vanish altogether as the river spilled over until it was three, four or five miles wide. A steamer might safely navigate where paddy had been cultivated the week before, yet run hard aground in a mid-river position and be stranded high and dry within hours. The GBM river system, untrained and with the numerous braiding channels present almost similar characteristics to the navigator even today.

Such hazards were never to be completely overcome and might well have defeated the pioneer navigators but, by the simple expedient of engaging local fishermen who knew every inch of their waters, they succeeded in establishing a system of pilotage which was to prove remarkably efficient. It was however, no less remarkable for its unique character and even today this system continues. The compass, landmark or celestial sightings were of little value where the navigable channel could pursue a course at 90° variance from the logical heading. Instead, the steamer commanders had to master the fishermen's art of 'reading' the water-detecting channels by the pattern of current flow, by the movement of water hyacinth on the surface, or even by the subtleties of light and shade in the muddy colours of the river waters.

Steamer Companies

Two companies; the India General Steam Navigation Company and the Rivers Steam Navigation Company combined forces and, under the banner of 'The Joint Steamer Companies', went on to create one of the largest ventures of its kind in the world. Hard on the heels of the pioneers, their little paddle steamers pushed out through. Bengal, the United Provinces and Assam, and the industrialisation of north-east India followed in their wake.

Long before India's first railway engine had steamed out of Bombay, the little ships had opened up the markets to trade, so laying the foundation of basic industry in the Bengal Presidency; they were to be the *raison d'être* for the country's first coal mines, the first ship-repair yards and the first rope-works; they carried the first bales of raw jute to the first jute mills in Calcutta and they carried into the Assam hinterland the men who opened up the first tea gardens which were to give the entire world a new beverage.

From the point of view of the navigator, the Ganges, the Brahmaputra and the Meghna have one feature in common, but they differ from one another in one important respect. The common feature is the fact that they all debouche into the plains at altitudes which are only a few hundred feet above sea level, although still many hundreds of miles from the sea. Consequently they become sluggish and during much of the year the pilot thus has to cope with constantly shifting shoals of sand. In the summer however, the snows of the high Himalayas melt and supplemented by the subsequent annual rains, the Ganges and Brahmaputra become raging torrents. They spill over their banks, but the force of the current is still sufficient to scour away all sandbanks (or chars, as they are called).

The difference between these two rivers and the Meghna arises from the fact that since the Meghna is not snow fed, in the early months of the year it falls to much lower levels than the Ganges or Brahmaputra. On the other hand, confined as it is to a deep gutter-like channel, it is more susceptible to dramatic rises of water level than the other two rivers. Navigation depths in the Meghna in the height of the annual rains season can attain as much as 10 metres; whereas a more normal depth on the broad reaches of the Brahmaputra would be from 3 to 4 metres. In the case of the Ganges where conditions must once have been similar to those on the Brahmaputra, its tributaries have been tapped over the years, either for irrigation purposes or for hydro-electric purposes and the navigational conditions deteriorated progressively to maximum depths of 1.5 to 2.5 metres.

Paddle Wheelers

In the early days the ships of the Ganges fleet were 'paddle wheelers' built of iron and were 100 feet long and 22 feet broad amid ship excluding paddle boxes. They had two engines each and were also rigged to carry sail. The steamers carried cargo and provided quarters for the officers, while `the accommodation barge for passengers and cargo was towed behind and in addition to the towing hawsers there was a broad beam of wood secured by a socket and pin on the front of the barge with a similar arrangement on the stern post of the tug, connecting the two vessels. This beam acted as a communicating gangway and also prevented the barge from colliding with the steamer when the latter ran aground. The accommodation barge was called a flat and had a fairly large saloon forward, with six to eight single cabins opening on to it. Cargo was stacked in the holds and on the after deck of the flat.

According to the season of the year, there were two possible routes from Calcutta to Allahabad. What might be called the all season route was down the Hooghly and then by a narrow channel, through the Sunderbans to Khulna and thence north into the Padma and on into the Ganges proper. In the rainy season it was also possible to steam from Calcutta up the Bhagirathi into the Ganges and so to avoid a great detour. It will be noted that the steamers were mainly employed on the service to Allahabad and not to Assam. The tea industry had not yet been established and there was little trade to be had from Assam, so that when steamers went to Assam, it was to meet the needs of the military or civil services. The direction of trade from Bengal was to the west, where Allahabad was the, most important town except for Delhi.

Roads between Calcutta and Delhi were in a bad state and moreover, they were still infested by thugs and dacoits. Travel by river might be slow, but it was at least preferable to the hazards of the highways. It was natural, therefore, that the first government steamers should be utilised on the Ganges.

Cachar Route

Towards the middle of 1800 the steamer companies turned their attention to Cachar, where the possibility of tea cultivation had recently been realised. Tea was in fact indigenous in Cachar, but it was only brought to notice in 1855 when F. Skipwith, a judge at Sylhet, sent specimens of Cachar tea down to the Agricultural and Horticultural Society in Calcutta. Little time was then lost by enterprising businessmen in following up this discovery. The first garden was opened in 1856; others followed quickly and by 1863 there was a considerable demand for the importation of labour and stores. In 1863, the IG (India General Steam Navigation Company) therefore despatched the vessel Agra on a voyage to Cachar. The establishment of a monthly service had been contemplated, but the experience of the first voyage showed that the shallowness of the Cachar rivers in the dry season created considerable difficulties and for some years the IG steamers only plied to Cachar in the rains. Fortunately that season more or less coincided with the busy season in the Tea Industry.

By 1873 about 73,000 acres of tea were under cultivation in Assam and transport between Calcutta and Assam had become the mainstay of the IG's business. The long journey through the Sunderbans was a handicap. In 1869, five years after the East Bengal Railway had been extended to Kushtia, the IG made a working arrangement with the. Railway by .which goods for Assam would be railed to Kushtia and transhipped there under through booking documents. For reasons which do not appear, this arrangement was abandoned in 1871, but by 1873 the railway had been extended to Goalundo and the importance of that point at the junction of three great rivers was obvious. It became one of the IG's most important stations and thenceforth, the normal route for passengers to Assam or East Bengal from

Calcutta was by train to Goalundo and thence by steamer.

With the fleet available as a result of the withdrawal from the Ganges, the steamer companies were able to introduce a regular service to Assam once in 10 days and also to develop a large and lucrative cargo trade with the great jute centres of East Bengal. Cachar continued to be served once a fortnight.

In 1885 the IG, again acting on its own, secured a contract for a despatch service to Cachar. In view of the difficulty of navigating the Cachar rivers in the dry season, special vessels of shallow draft were required. Eight such steamers were acquired, but they could only start from Narayanganj since the coaching traffic between Goalundo and Narayanganj was still preserve of the Railway. The terminus of the service was Fenchuganj, but the IG also put a vessel on to link Fenchuganj with the important business centre, Karimganj.

Half a century was to pass before changed traffic patterns, induced by the Partition of India, created a demand for bulk cargo movements over the deep and relatively straight reaches of river between Khulna and Narayanganj. Only then did push-towing become feasible. It was also only at this late stage in the Companies' history that technical developments on screw propulsion became sufficiently advanced to provide adequate protection against damage, so making shallow water operation by screw driven vessels a more practicable proposition.

Innovations and Fleet Expansion

Nonetheless, by the closing decade of the 19th century the Companies had already established that screw propulsion was considerably more efficient than paddle drive for deep water operation and virtually all vessels thereafter constructed for exclusive operation in such waters were screw propelled.

Technical innovations were made for river conservancy. The rivers of Bengal bring down large quantities of silt and either deposit it on the bank or allow it to raise the bed and create sandbanks and shoals here and there. Dredging is thus essential., but unfortunately it is a costly process. Apparently it was not until the 20th century that the Governments of Bengal and Assam rather grudgingly began to recognise that they had as much responsibility for the maintenance of channels in the principal rivers as for the upkeep of highways. The steamer companies were in fact left to cope with this problem for themselves and in 1903 they purchased a dredging plant which was fitted on to the Nemotha. Dredging was done through a suction head and discharge pipes.

River conservancy involves not only dredging but bandalling—and establishing marks and buoys. A bandal consists of a framework of bamboos driven into the river bed and buttressed by bamboo struts. To this framework are tied mats made of bamboo splits. Bandals can be laid to cause silt to be deposited in order to close a minor channel and divert water into the main channel or to deflect the main current away from an eroding bank.

Even with many additions the fleets were not adequate for the rapidly increasing traffic. Not only were the tea and jute industries growing apace they were also acting as priming pumps for commerce generally. Tea, jute and inland water transport were in fact bringing new life to Assam and East Bengal and there was close correlation between the growth of these three major industries and that of the Railways.

The opportunities were plenty and the steamer companies continued to augment their fleets in carefully considered relation to the expected growth of traffic. In the decade preceding the First World War, the two British Companies between them constructed over 39 flats and barges, 32 despatch and mail steamers, 12 towing steamers and many smaller craft. When war broke out, the IG fleet thus consisted of 113 steamers, 18 tugs and launches, 185 flats and 138 cargo boats. The RSN fleet at this time consisted of 117 steamers, 22 tugs and launches, 171 flats, 50 cargo boats and 23 miscellaneous craft.

Set Back to IWT

On 24th September 1919 a hurricane swept across the Sunderbans and on to Khulna, Narayanganj and Dacca and then blew itself out in the Khasia hills. It was accompanied by a great tidal wave which carried many vessels over the river bed and deposited them in paddy fields. Sixteen or seventeen of the Joint Companies' vessels were sunk, but luckily a large number of them was in shallow water at the time and were salvaged easily. Over 130 vessels were damaged, but as in the case of earlier cyclones, the ultimate loss was not as great as had been feared.

Until 1949 all rail and river traffic between Assam and Calcutta had passed through Pakistan, but in that year the Government of India set themselves to construct a railway line which would be entirely within India, just north of East Bengal. This involved the construction of over a hundred bridges and the formidable task of bridging the swift-running glacier-fed river Tista. This involved realigning the original Calcutta—Assam route further north into the foothills of the Dooars over exceedingly difficult terrain, with the rail track at right angles to the natural drainage of the land. From the point of view of the Joint Companies, this posed a new threat. Fortunately, as it would seem to them, the capacity of the line was limited and whenever political conditions permitted, the river steamers continued to be the main means of transport between Assam and Calcutta.

When hostilities broke out, the borders between India and Pakistan were at once closed. About a third of the Indian fleet, which now operated under the Central Inland Water Transport Corporation, was trapped in East Pakistan and seized by the Government of that Province as enemy property—and was not returned when the fighting came to an end. Another third of the fleet was trapped in Assam and unable to pass through Pakistan to Calcutta and most of these vessels were in due course scrapped. When the river route was reopened in 1972 after the secession of Bangladesh, the only remaining elements of the fleet were vessels which had been in Calcutta when war began. These were altogether inadequate for the restoration of the old services and moreover the vast back-up organisation of cargo stations, conservancy, pilotage and workshops—was no longer in existence. The services which were resumed were mainly restricted to the Calcutta–Bangladesh routes. There were no voyages to Cachar and only an occasional voyage to Assam.

By 1860,the extension of East Indian Railways had begun to make itself felt. The decline of inland navigation, in fact began with the construction of railways in 1855 to start with the construction of main lines gave a spurt to river traffic as a feeder route to the railways. The construction of branch lines and lines parallel to the river robbed the steamers and boats of their traffic even though they were cheaper as compared to road and rail. The water transport was not properly organised and was not given the support by the government as was given to the other modes. The proliferation of irrigation projects and the large withdrawals of water from the dry water supplies of the river was another cause of deterioration of navigability in the upper reaches of the rivers. Even in the present context these two issues are relevant for the revival of the river transport.

Indo Bangladesh Cooperation

Globally there is a felt need for the revival of the river transport. Many developed and developing countries are making huge investments for the systematic up gradation of the waterways and water transport. Both India and Bangladesh have ambitious projects for the sustainable development of the inland water transport system. Two major land marks in the revival of navigation in the GBM routes are the Indo-Bangladesh Trade Agreement of March 1972 and the Indo-Bangladesh Protocol in October 1972l on Inland Water Transit and Trade. These bilateral agreements facilitated transit of vessels and inter-country trade from Ports of Calls in India and Bangladesh. In 2010-11 more than 300 Bangladesh vessels have operated in the protocol route moving over 1.3 million tonnes of cargo. The Ashuganj-Karimganj routes, the focus of the present study, is important, both in terms of transit and inter-country traffic between India and Bangladesh and intra-Bangladesh transportation in the Meghna-Surma Kushiara region.

References and Acknowldgement.

1) A History of the Joint Steamer Companies by Sir Percival Griffiths, K.B.C.I.E., 1979.

2) Navigable Waterways of India, CWPC, 1961.

3) Contributions by Inland Navigators of CIWTC, IWT Assam.

ANNEX-3

Protocol on Inland Water Transit and Trade

In pursuance of Article VIII of the Trade Agreement entered into between the Government of the People's Republic of Bangladesh and the Government of the Republic of India on the 9th February, 2009, wherein the two Governments agreed to make mutually beneficial arrangements for the use of their waterways for commerce between the two countries for passage of goods between two places in one country through the territory of the other, in accordance with the laws of the country through the territory of which goods are moving, it is further agreed as following:

1. Definition:

For the purpose of this Protocol unless the context otherwise requires:

1.1 The term "Competent Authorities" will mean the authorities authorized by the respective Government:

1.2 The term "route" will refer to the routes:

(1) Kolkata-Haldia-Raimongal-Chalna-Khulna-Mongla-Kaulhali-Barisal-Hizla-Chandpur-Narayangonj-Aricha-Sirajganj-Bahadurabad-Chilmari-Dhubri-Pandu-Shilghat.

(2) Shilghat-Pandu-Dhubri-Chimari-Bahadurabad-Sirajganj-Aricha-Narayangonj-Chandpur-Hizla-Barisal-Kaulhali-Mongla-Khuna-Chalna-Raimongal-Haldia-Kolkata.

(3) Kolkata-Haldia-Raimongal-Mongla-Kaukhali-Barisal-Hizla-Chandpur-Narayangonj-Bhairab Bazar-Ashuganj-Ajmiriganj-Markuli-Sherpur-Fenchuganj-Zakiganj-Karimganj.

(4) Karimganj-Zakiganj-Fenchuganj-Sherpur-Markuli-Ajmiriganj-Ashuganj-Bhairab Bazar-Narayangonj-Chandpur-Hizla-Barisal-Kaukhali-Mongla-Raimongal-Haldia-Kolkata.

(5) Rajshahi-Godagari-Dhulian.

(6) Dhulian-Godagari-Rajshahi.

(7) Karimganj-Zakiganj-Fenchuganj-Sherpur-Markuli-Ajmiriganj-Ashuganj-Bhairab Bazar-Narayangonj-Chandpur-Aricha-Sirajganj-Bahadurabad-Chilmari-Dhubri-Pandu-Shilghat.

(8) Shilghat-Pandu-Dhubri-Chilmari-Bahadurabad-Sirajganj-Aricha-Chandpur-Narayangonj-Bhairab Bazar-Ashuganj-Ajmiriganj-Markuli-Sherpur-Fenchuganj-Zakiganj-Karimganj—or such other routes as may be prescribed by the Competent Authorities from time to time.

1.3 The term "Vessels" will mean the watercrafts which are registered under the Inland Shipping Ordinance, 1976 as amended from time to time in case of Bangladesh vessels and Inland Vessels

1.4 Act, 1917, as amended from time to time in case of Indian Vessels. This will cover vessels which carry only commercial goods stated in the preamble of the Protocol.

2. Conservancy and Pilotage:

2.1 Each country will maintain the river routes falling within its territory in a navigable condition and provide all the essential pilotage and conservancy services, including hydrographic surveys and supply of charts, if prepared and available for commercial navigational use to inland water transport operators, and aids to night navigation where facilities for such navigation already exist.

2.2 Acknowledging that there may be routes or parts of routes in one country, primarily being used by the transit traffic of the other, the country maintaining such routes will provide aids to night navigation on such routes, provided the country using such routes pays, by mutual agreement, for the installation and maintenance of such aids. The amount to be paid and the manner of its payment shall be mutually agreed upon by the two sides.

3. Port Dues and Other Charges:

3.1 Port dues may be levied by the competent authorities in either country on the vessels belonging to the other country and engaged in inter-country trade.

3.2 The competent authorities in either country may also levy on the vessels of the other country charges for conservancy, pilotage and other specific services at par with those charged from the local vessels. The charges will be determined with reference to cargo carrying capacity of the vessels, as applicable to local vessels.

3.3 Acknowledging that one country may be required to maintain routes or parts of routes primarily on account of the transit traffic of the other, the country utilizing such routes will provide to the other country an agreed sum of money for the maintenance of such routes including conservancy and pilotage.

3.4 The routes between Sirajganj and Daikhawa in the Northern Delta Section of the River Jamuna-Brahamaputra and the route between Sherpur and Zakiganj in the North Eastern Delta Section of the Kushiyara river are recognized by both sides as routes being maintained primarily for the use of Indian transit traffic.

3.5 For the maintenance of the above mentioned services on these routes, the Government of India has been paying to the Government of Bangladesh in convertible currency at the rate of BD taka 200 Lakh per year till 23rd March, 2009. It was agreed that an upward revision of these rates will be considered by the Government of India in consultation with the Government of Bangladesh.

4. Handling Facilities:

Each country will permit the vessels of the other country to utilize all available cranes and other handling facilities on the same terms and conditions as are applicable to local vessels.

5. Supply of Bunkers:

The vessels of either country plying between the two countries and also between places in the same country through the other country will be permitted to purchase the fuel required by them for the purpose of their operations on payment in convertible currency. Inland vessels registered in Bangladesh may be bunkered at Kolkata, Budge-Budge, Haldia, Karimganj, Dhubri and Pandu in India. Likewise, vessels registered in India may be bunkered at Mongla industrial belt, Khulna, Barisal, Chandpur, Narayangonj and Sirajganj in Bangladesh. Any alteration/addition in respect of bunkering points may be decided through mutual consultations.

6. Purchase of Essential Stores:

The vessels operating in either country will be allowed to purchase in convertible currency the stores which they may require for their operation during the voyage in the other country at places of bunkering. In order to do so, conversion facilities will be provided at the bunkering points.

7. Purchase of Provisions by the Fleet Personnel during Voyage:

Fresh food and other provisions essential for fleet personnel will be allowed to be purchased in either country to meet the requirements of voyage. The purchase will be made in convertible currency at the points of bunkering. In order to do so, conversion facilities will be provided at the bunkering points. In exceptional circumstances only purchases may be made at places other than the bunkering points. The appropriate authorities of either country may prescribe the manner in which such purchases may be made should it be deemed necessary.

8. Repair Facilities:

Vessels of either country calling for urgent repairs en route will be allowed to have repairs done at the Government owned and/or public sector marine workshop in either country. The expenditure incurred on such repairs will be reported by the operators to the concerned foreign exchange authorities for their clearance in accordance with the provisions of Article 25.

9. Assistance to be provided by either Country to the Vessels of the Other in Distress :

Each country will provide all the necessary facilities to the vessels of the other, which may be grounded or otherwise in distress during their voyage in its waterways. Expenditure incurred in salvage operations, if required on such occasions, shall be cleared in accordance with the arrangements to be made under Article 25.

10. Submission of Voyage Forecast for Voyage Permission to Use Waterways:

The vessels of one country before using the waterways of the other country will obtain the permission of the other country for entry. In such cases the voyage forecasts, in the prescribed form, for the vessels of one country will be submitted to the competent authority of the other county at least four days before the expected date of entry into the country of entry.

11. Nomination of "Ports of Call" on Equal Basis:

One country will provide the facilities of "Ports of Call" to the vessels of the other country engaged in inter-country trade and number of such Ports of Call will be equal in both countries. Both sides agreed that the following would be treated as 'Ports of Call' in their respective country.

Bangladesh	India
Narayaganj	Kolkata
Khulna	Haldia
Mongla	Karimganj
Sirajganj	Pandu
Ashuganj	Shilghat

12. Recognition of Survey Certificates and Other Documents:

The survey certificates and other documents issued by the appropriate authorities in one country for the vessels registered in it and running to or through the other will be recognized and accepted as valid by the other. These certificates or documents shall be produced by the Master of the vessels concerned at the points of entry and at the other points, as may be required, during the voyage.

13. Flying of Flags:

The vessels of each country will carry its national flag and the national flag of the country through which it is transiting besides its house flag.

14. Use of Radio-Telephone by River Craft:

Inland vessels will be allowed to be equipped with radio-telephone for facilities of speedy commercial communications, especially in emergencies, in conformity with the current regulations of the country through which the vessels are in transit.

15. Registration and Issue of Identity Cards:

The personnel manning vessels plying through or between the two countries shall carry certificate of employment and permits with a photograph of the concerned individual duly authenticated by the authorities to be nominated by the respective countries in regard to their personnel. Officers supervising or controlling the fleet of the operators in either country shall carry passport endorsed with multiple entry visas.

16. Permission to Fleet Personnel and Traveling Officers to go by Rail, Road of Air in Special Circumstances:

Fleet personnel and traveling officers posted to any of the vessels carrying transit cargo in either country will be allowed to travel by rail, road or air, whenever they are required to join duty on the vessels, or when they have to leave their duty on the vessels by reason of sickness of other urgent contingencies. Such movements will be simultaneously reported to the appropriate authorities of either country.

17. Prohibition on Vessels Carrying Transit Cargo:

Vessels carrying transit cargo through one country will not be engaged in inter-country trade and will not take or discharge cargo or passengers in the country through which they are passing. All necessary facilities for inspection will be accorded by each country to the Customs and other agencies. No undue delay will be caused to the voyage of any vessels on account of such inspections.

18. Sharing of Inter-country Trade and Transit Cargo:

The two Governments agree to sharing of the carriage of inter-country trade and transit cargo on an equal tonnage basis (i.e. 50:50) by the vessels of signatory countries to and from ports of call/customs stations including extended places of loading and unloading under customs formalities and supervision. The competent authorities of the two countries will take steps to operationalise the sharing through appropriate measures keeping in view that expeditious transportation of cargo is in the mutual interest of both countries.

19. Common Freight Rates:

The operators in both the countries will charge to the extent practicable uniform freight rates for both inter-country trade and transit traffic. Such rates will be fixed by the competent authorities by mutual consultations.

20. Evolving Uniform Documentation for Vessels:

The document issued in accordance with the regulations in one country, in respect of the cargoes carried by vessels going to or through the other country will be accepted by the other. Efforts will be made to evolve uniform documentation in both the countries as early as possible.

A Manifest in duplicate for in-transit goods in addition to the Manifest Book shall be submitted to the Customs Officer at the point of entry. One copy of the Manifest will be retained by him and the other, duly endorsed will be sent in sealed cover through the Master of the vessel to the Customs Officer at the exit points.

21. Customs Checks and Documentation:

Both the countries agree to reduce customs documentation and other requirements to the essential minimum for the purpose of transit and to have custom stations at or near the points of entry and exit in each country.

22. Freight Remittance Facilities:

The freight earned by the vessels of either country from the traffic, originating in the other and carried by them, will be allowed to be remitted to the owners of the vessels in accordance with the arrangements for remittance of surplus collection between the two countries that may be in force from time to time in accordance with Article 25.

23. Permission to Operate Trucks between Places in India and River Stations in Bangladesh:

23.1 Bangladesh truck and/or tractor-trailers may carry cargoes trans-shipped from river crafts at Sherpur and Ashuganj to the Indian border.

23.2 Cargoes brought by deeper draft vessels from India up to Sherpur or any other point on the waterways in Bangladesh may be trans-shipped into shallow draft vessels for destination in India. Conversely, trans-shipments can also be made from shallow draft vessels to deeper draft vessels. Trans-shipments will be carried out under the supervision of BIWTA and Customs authorities of Bangladesh.

24. Opening of Branch Offices and Appointment of Agents:

The operators of vessels in one country will be allowed to open their branch offices or appoint their agents only at major inland ports and secondary river ports in the other. However, such branch offices will be opened with due approval from the country concerned.

25. Arrangements for Settlement, Clearance & Remittance:

Subject to their respective foreign exchange regulations, the competent authorities of Bangladesh and India, shall through mutual consultations, establish a comprehensive system for quick settlement, clearance and remittance of all sums, claims, or dues on account of goods supplied, services rendered or facilities accorded to the vessels of one country in or by the other.

26. Setting-up of a Standing Committee:

For evaluation and reviewing the working of this Protocol and for the purpose of improvement of inland water transportation between the two countries, there shall be a Standing Committee, including representatives of the Ministry of Shipping of Bangladesh and the Ministry of Shipping, Road Transport and Highways, Department of Shipping of India, the representatives of the Ministry of Finance of Bangladesh and of India, the representatives of BIWTA and BIWTC of Bangladesh and IWAI and CIWTC of India, the concerned customs officials of both countries and two representatives of the operators one from each country.

The Committee may co-opt members whose participation is considered necessary by it. The Standing Committee shall meet at least once in six months and its findings shall be forwarded to the respective Governments for necessary action.

27. Addition of New Routes and more Ports of Call:

Additional routes and new ports of call may be added through an addendum to this Protocol by mutual consultation between the two countries.

28. Term of the Protocol:

This Protocol shall come into force from the 1st April 2009 and shall remain in force up to 31st March 2011. It may be extended for a further period through mutual consent subject to such modifications as may be agreed upon.